Don Ellison's

CAMELLIAS

A Photo Dictionary

Don Ellison's

CAMELLIAS

A Photo Dictionary

C. japonica 'Thomas Walter Savige'[1]

Author **Don Ellison**

Consultant Editor **Thomas J. Savige**

Flora Publications International Pty Ltd

National Library of Australia Cataloguing-in-Publication
  Ellison, Donald Phillip 1934-
     Don Ellison's Camellias—A Photo Dictionary
     Includes index
     ISBN 1 876060 01 8 (Camellias)
     1. Camellia. 2. Camellia - Identification. 3. Camellia - Pictorial Works. I. Title.
       583.264

A Flora Publications Book
First Published 1997

Photographs and text (except where acknowledged)
© Don Ellison

Additional text (except where acknowledged), artwork, concept and design
© Flora Publications International Pty Ltd

Book Design by CopyRight Publishing Company Pty Ltd

Colour reproductions by Graphic Skills Pty Ltd

Printed in Brisbane Queensland Australia by HBM Print Pty Ltd

Flora Publications International Pty Ltd
371 Queen Street / GPO Box 2927
Brisbane Queensland Australia 4001
Telephone +61 7 3229 6906
Facsimile +61 7 3229 8782
Email info@flora.com.au

C. japonica 'Carter's Sunburst'

I dedicate this book to my sister, Nell Haigh, who has grown, exhibited and loved camellias for more than 50 years. Her favourites are illustrated herewith.

C. japonica 'Desire'

I would like to thank the many nursery owners, camellia growers, camellia exhibitors and curators of botanical gardens throughout the world for affording me the opportunity to take the photographs used in this book.

My thanks also go to the following people who cross-checked the photographs used:- Azalea Grove Nursery, Cowell's Camellia Nursery, Camellia Grove Nursery, Tom Savige and Denerley Woolley.

I also wish to thank Tom Savige[1], Cowell's Nursery[2], Dr Withers[3], Nuccio's Nursery[4], Jim Pinkerton[5], Denerley Woolley[6], Dr Ackerman[7] and Bob Cherry[8] for supplying some of the photographs used. Photographs are tagged as numbered herewith for these individual contributors.

My thanks go also to Paul Niederer who, in consultation with James Sokoll, developed a system for processing the technical data which allowed efficient cross checking and provided layouts needed to complete this major work in a short time frame, and to Melinda Sampson for her exceptional efforts in scanning, colour correction and layout.

CONTENTS

Foreword

While Camellias have been grown and appreciated for over 500 years in China and Japan it was only 250 years ago that this genus became known to the Western World. Lord Petre, a patron of the Jesuit missionaries in China, is thought to have received the first camellias to reach the west, from returning missionaries, as he had plants growing at his Thorndon Hall in about 1739. However it was not until the last decade of the 18th century that garden camellias began to arrive in England from China and were mostly given names in Latin, such as 'Alba Plena'; 'Althaeiflora' and 'Variegata'. These soon became distributed to America and other European countries. It was not long before plant breeders had taken them up and new cultivars made their appearance, bred by such men as Chandler and Curtis in England; Luzzatti and Rovelli in Italy, Hovey and Floy in America, Loureiro in Portugal, not to forget Macarthur in Australia. Soon camellias were in every garden; some nurseries listing up to 1,000 varieties. The formal doubles were the most popular and we find the Verschaffelts illustrating 623 cultivars without including a flower of single or semi-double form.

By the end of the 19th century, interest in the genus waned in the Western World, probably due to lack of variety. For the first 30 years of the 20th century nurseries in the West listed very few camellias. In Australia 'Alba Plena', 'Pink Perfection', 'Great Eastern' and 'Emperor of Russia' were the main ones grown.

The modern camellia era began in the late 1930s, with a resurgence of interest in the USA which resurrected many of the old cultivars as well as importing others from England, Portugal and Japan. As the true identification of many of the old cultivars was lost, this led to a period of nomenclature confusion and considerable attention was given to this problem by the newly formed American Camellia Society and Southern California Camellia Society. The latter was formed about 1944 and began the regular production of the publication now known as *Camellia Nomenclature*. The Australia Camellia Research Society under the guidance of the late Professor E. G. Waterhouse was also very active in the research into old camellia names.

In 1957 The Longwood Foundation of America made a substantial grant towards investigation into camellia nomenclature. This was administered by the L. H. Bailey Hortorium of the Cornel University and led to the formation of a project advisory group who became the foundation for the International Camellia Society in 1962. In 1958 the first edition of *The International Code of Nomenclature for Cultivated Plants* was published and its rules were accepted world-wide. The newly formed International Camellia Society became the Registration Authority for the Genus Camellia in 1962.

The ensuing, considerable, general interest in camellias led to extensive hybridizing and the production of new cultivars. This was accelerated by the introduction of the Kunming reticulatas, and soon the hybridizers had a new generation of these magnificent cultivars, crosses with *Camellia japonica*. This cross produced plants hardier and of a better form and more suitable to the garden. Nurseries were soon listing reticulata hybrids like 'Arch of Triumph', 'William Hertrich', 'Valley Knudsen', 'Lasca Beauty', 'Arcadia' and many more as well the original Kunming reticulatas such as 'Juban', 'Cornelian', 'Pagoda', 'Crimson Robe' etc.

While a few other camellia species had arrived in the West in the past, such as *C. rosiflora, C. maliflora, C. cuspidata* and *C. sasanqua*, suddenly, as China opened its doors to the West, a flood of new species started to arrive from the late 1970s and on. These included the scented *C. lutchuensis*, the miniature flowered *C. transnokoensis*, and *C, transarisensis*, the wavy leaved

C. tsaii, C. yunnanensis and *C. granthamiana* with their large centre of stamens, *C. fraterna* and others. This was capped in 1979 by the introduction of the first member of the yellow flowered group, *C. nitidissima*. The hybridists are having a 'field day', out of which have already emerged two new groups of camellia cultivars, the scented camellias and the miniature cluster flowering hybrids. Most of the scented camellia cultivars have *C. lutchuensis* in their ancestry. Two of the first were 'Cinnamon Cindy' and 'Fragrant Pink'. Others include 'Fragrant Joy', 'High Fragrance', 'Spring Mist', 'Scented Gem' and 'Scentuous'. The cluster flowering miniatures were bred from a mixture including two or more of the following species; *C. fraterna*, for mass flowering, *C. rosiflora*, for pink colouring, *C. tsaii* for wavy edged leaves, *C. cuspidata* for tall growth, *C. transnokoensis* and *C. nokoensis* for fine leaved foliage and 'Kurotsubaki' for deep, dark red colouring. Amongst these cultivars are 'Baby Willow', 'Fairy Wand', 'Gay Baby', 'Wirlinga Princess', 'Wirlinga Bride', 'Snowdrop', 'Alpen Glo' and many more.

National registration authorities have been set up in USA, Australia and New Zealand to control this flood of new cultivars and illustrated books are regularly published to show them. Many of the early ones were of paintings, the latter ones of coloured photographs. These illustrated works started in the early 19th century and included the monumental publications of Verschaffelt and Berlése with their hand coloured illustrations. Some of the more modern books include Waterhouse's *Camellia Quest* and *Camellia Trail*, now collectors' items; Hume's *Camellias in America*; Hertrich's *Camellias in the Huntington Gardens*; the more modern Macoboy's *The Colour Dictionary of Camellias*; Rolfe's *Gardening with Camellias* and Durrant's *The Camellia Story*.

The continued production of such works is most desirable to assist in identification and to stabilise nomenclature and is more than ever necessary today with its average annual production of 250 new cultivars. As Ambroise Verschaffelt says in his introduction to his *Nouvelle Iconographie des Camellias*: 'It is the intention to give to posterity a description and perfect illustration in the true colours of those varieties not previously described, which are considered as having sufficient merit to warrant perpetuation.'

Don Ellison is to be congratulated on the production of this publication which is worthy successor to those that have gone before.

Thomas J. Savige
International Registrar of the Genus Camellia
24th February 1997

Camellia Forms

Single form
C. japonica 'Tama-no-ura'

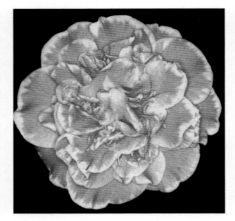

Peony form
C. japonica 'Jean Clere'

Pendulous flowers
C. japonica 'Kujaku'

Formal double form
C. japonica 'Red Red Rose'

Anemone form
C. japonica 'C. M. Wilson'

Fimbriated petals
C. japonica 'Fimbriata'

Semi-double form
C. japonica 'Grand Prix'

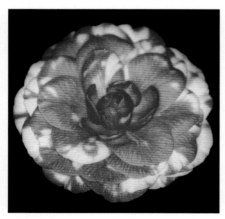

Rose form
C. japonica 'Dee Davis Variegated'

Variegated foliage
C. japonica 'Benten'

Colour and Form Variations—

Camellia flowers are known to vary widely, from climate to climate and from soil type to soil type. Those grown in a dry climate or sandy soil usually are much paler in colour than those grown in heavy soils or where climates are humid. The variation can be seen in both flowers and flower forms.

The illustrations below of *C. japonica* 'Margaret Davis' are examples of these variations.

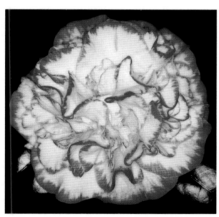

C. japonica 'Margaret Davis'
Photographed in Atlanta, USA.

C. japonica 'Margaret Davis'
Photographed in Sydney, Australia.

Photo Dictionary layout

The aim of this dictionary is to present a visual display of a large variety of camellias in cultivation around the world, presented so as to enable the reader to readily identify each species and to gain a basic awareness of the flower form, colour and general characteristics of each plant. Plants are listed according to species (e.g. *Camellia japonica*), or type (e.g. Camellia hybrids), and within each different classification plants are listed alphabetically—however the predominant species, *C.japonica*, is depicted first in the photo dictionary.

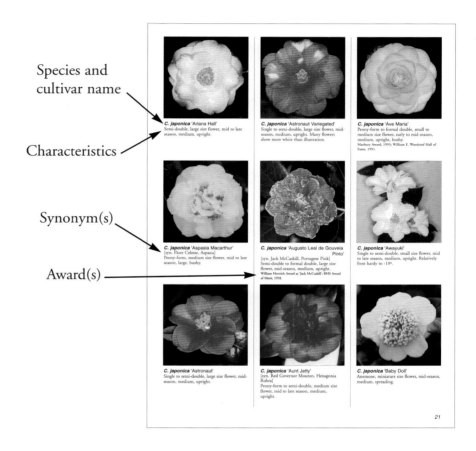

Species and cultivar name

Characteristics

Synonym(s)

Award(s)

Index layout

Three indices are provided. The first lists species and cultivar, but with *C. japonica* placed in its alphabetic sequence.

The second lists the most commonly used synonyms. The genetic '*C.*' has been disregarded in terms of the alphabetical ordering of this list.

The third, the comprehensive index, is a list of all names and synonyms, again excluding the genetic '*C.*'.

Introduction

Most of the photographs used in this book were taken over a period of 27 years, during my visits to countries which included U.S.A., England, Ireland, France, Japan, Italy, Holland, Belgium, New Zealand, and travels throughout Australia. Up to 15 photographs were taken of each cultivar and on many occasions a cultivar may have been photographed in all of the above countries. I have taken over 20,000 photographs of more than 2,000 different camellias and it was a difficult job to select the pictures to be used.

Many cultivars had wide colour variations from country to country and from state to state. To get the best possible final colour for the book, the first selection criterion used was to choose the photograph which best matched the registered colour of each plant.

I found that flowers from gardens like Savill Gardens in England were much deeper in colour than flowers from Los Angeles or Sydney which have drier soil and much more sunlight. The flowers in Auckland were usually the closest to the average colour.

Soil types also played a big part in both colour and size of the flowers as did the type of fertilizer used.

At one large camellia show I attended there were 12 entries in the *C. reticulata* section for cv. Dr Clifford Parks, and every flower was a different size and a different shade of red.

Propagation

I first started propagating camellias in 1956 in a nursery and garden centre in Nowra, Australia, and over the next 20 years had propagated more than 1 million camellia plants.

My target result was between 95% and 100% strike rate and this was usually achieved with most cultivars.

Over the years I have spoken to many nursery people, enthusiastic gardeners and growers who strike camellias and I would say that, for every 100 propagators, there are 100 variations to the method used. Some vary widely, whilst other variations are only small.

Professional growers now mostly use fog or mist with bottom heat, and with just these two factors in propagation there is a wide variation about the heating temperature, method of heating, duration of fogging or misting and type of switch mechanism used.

Other variables which play important roles in striking cuttings are the propagating mixture, when the cutting is taken, and how the cutting is treated.

I have seen propagators take their cuttings at any time during spring, summer, autumn and even winter with varying success rates—I can only conclude that if you have a good success rate, stick with what you are doing.

My most successful method of production was to take cuttings during the last two weeks of spring and the first two weeks of summer, at this time the wood of the camellia cuttings was semi-mature. The cuttings would be usually cut with very sharp secateurs below the 5th or 6th leaf from the top, the 2 or 3 lower leaves would then be removed and the top three leaves cut in half. The cuttings would then be washed in a mixture of water and bleach at a rate 50 ml bleach to 10 litres of tap water.

It is necessary that the secateurs be washed with a water/bleach mix at the rate of 50/50 after each lot of cuttings is taken from a plant, as the sap from a virus-variegated plant can be transferred on the secateurs if the secateurs are not cleaned. It may cause a cutting of a virus-free plant to become a virus-variegated plant. Disease can also be transmitted from one plant to another on secateurs.

Mixture

The propagating mixture which I found to be the most successful was 1/3 peat moss, 1/3 coarse Perlite and 1/3 washed, coarse, river sand.

I prefer to sterilize the mix, but if the sand is good quality, it may not be necessary. Sterilization can be carried out with Methyl Bromide gas, Formulin or heat treatment at 130°F for 10 minutes. Small batches can be treated in a microwave for 3 to 4 minutes, and the mixture then put into small plastic tubes or liners which have good drainage.

Cuttings are dipped into medium grade hormone rooting powder and then placed into the tubes of mix and lightly watered with a very fine hose head. Difficult-to-strike camellias such as *C. reticulata* benefit from double dipping. To double dip, first dip the cuttings into a liquid hormone solution such as 'Easiroot', leave for about one minute, then dip into the hormone powder.

My propagating bed consisted of electric cables for bottom heat set at 75°F or 240°C. A mist unit was used with the mist coming on for 10 seconds, 8 times during daylight hours.

For gardeners who only want to grow a few plants from cuttings the bottom two-thirds of a large, plastic, soft drink bottle makes a good mini-greenhouse and if similar propagating mix is used in a pot, the bottom of the bottle is then placed over the cuttings and watered from time to time.

If you intend to exhibit or want outstanding blooms, an important factor on selecting cuttings is to pick out the best flower on the plant and mark this place with a piece of string or a twisty tie. The new growth above this is the best cutting to use and should give you flowers similar to the one you marked. If a cutting is taken from the branch of a poor flower, you can expect the resultant plant to have poor flowers.

Mutations

Mutations, or sports, as they are called, are branches where the flowers vary in shape or colour from the other flowers of your camellia plant. If this flowering branch is then marked and a cutting taken from the new shoot above the flower, you should then have a new cultivar from this plant. Mutations can be forced artificially by using Colchicine which is a chemical made from colchicum bulbs.

Colchicine can be purchased from chemist supply stores or can be made by extracting the sap from a colchicum bulb. The sap is mixed with water at 50%. To apply, cut a camellia leaf bud about 6 leaves down on a new shoot in the spring and place a drop of Colchicine/water mix in the wound. In about 8 to 12 weeks time, take the shoot just above where the wound was made and propagate that shoot. The resultant plant may become a new cultivar. Some growers put a colchacine drop in the area where the bud was removed every 2 weeks.

Growing Camellias

Outstanding camellias can be grown very successfully if a few rules are observed. Firstly, the soil needs to be a little acid, with the ideal pH reading to be about 6.5. Camellias will grow in soils with more acid than this or even in soils neutral to very slightly alkaline. When camellias grow in very acid soils, they sometimes suffer yellowing because they are not able to absorb trace elements and on these occasions it is beneficial, every three months, to give a heavy watering with a mixture of 1 teaspoon of iron chelates and 5 teaspoons of *Magnesium sulphate* (Epsom Salts) to a standard size watering can.

The soil for most camellias needs to be an open, humus-enriched soil which has good drainage. *C. sasanqua*, *C. vernalis* and *C. hiemalis* are more tolerant of poorer soils and will tolerate full sun and windy situations.

Most of the other camellias especially japonicas, reticulatas and most hybrids prefer a sheltered situation away from winds and in a semi-shaded or morning-sun type area.

When camellias become too bushy, they will respond to a heavy pruning and if grown for exhibition purposes both pruning and disbudding need to be carried out to get the best blooms.

New Cultivars

Over the last 40 years many thousands of new cultivars have become available, with well chosen breeding programmes being undertaken as new species forms are collected by nurserymen and breeders. The combinations seem endless, with many new colours, shapes, fragrance and cold tolerance expected.

The yellow flowered *C. nitidissima* is one camellia which has been widely used in the last few years to endeavour to have yellow coloured flowers in all of the camellia flower forms.

Camellia Pests and Diseases

Camellias are regarded as being among Nature's hardier plant types, and are relatively free of pests and diseases when compared to other plants. When grown in good, well-drained soil, they should not need a lot of care and attention, but disease may enter the plant after severe pruning, or damage caused by hail storms, strong winds or moving the plant.

Diseases

Dieback (*Clomerella cingulata*) is one such disease which may arise from such damage as above, and may also be spread by sap-sucking insects or splashes of soil caused by heavy rain. It is most prevalent in *C. japonica* and *C. sasanqua*. It is identified by the wilting and death of new growth, and cankers forming on dead branches. Some control may be given by cutting back, hard, the infected branches and then spraying with Captan and Benlate. If the infected branches are removed, the secateurs should be sterilized in a mixture of laundry bleach, 50% to water, for at least one minute.

Root rot (*Phytophthora cinnamomi*) is soil or water borne, and infects plants through the roots. It is a disease common to many plants, and can be carried in soil, on the shoes, or spread by untreated irrigation water from dams. The first signs are seen in the form of yellowing leaves. If *C. sasanqua* or *C. oleifera* are used as rootstock when grafting, root rot can be overcome. A drench using Fongarid and Terrachlor to unaffected plants should stop the spread of this disease.

Camellia Flower Blight is a relatively new disease to the western world, and not yet found in all camellia growing areas. There does not appear to be any total control available yet, and it is mostly seen late in the season.

Flowers are badly marked with brown spots, and it is advisable to remove and burn all flowers from plants towards the end of the season, to minimize the risk of infection.

Insects

Aphids are the most likely insects to attack camellias, and are usually found on the new growth, or around the buds. They excrete a sticky substance like honey, which may, in turn, attract ants. Sprays such as Malathion or Metasystox, used only at the strength shown on the bottle, will control aphids.

Thrips are occasionally found on camellia flowers, and can cause unsightly white marks on the petals, which can also be twisted. Control of these almost invisible insects can be achieved by spraying with Malathion or Metasystox.

Mites are very small insect pests which are hard to see. If in large numbers, the mites will cause bud-balling, which may in turn cause brown marks on the outer edge of the petals. Control is by spraying with red spider oil.

Scale is occasionally another problem found on camellias, usually on the leaves. There are various types of scale:- wax, red, camellia, peony, and tea scale, and the name 'scale' comes from the scaly or waxy shell which covers the small insect.

There are many oil sprays which are used to control scale. These sprays need to be mixed with Diazinon or Malathion for best results.

Spraying should take place in the late afternoon, as leaves can get sun-burn if they are sprayed in the hotter part of the day. Two sprayings may be needed, 6 weeks apart, to control scale. Best results are obtained in late spring.

Voices of experience

Personal Experiences In Camellia Breeding Over The Years

by William L. Ackerman*

My first exposure to camellia breeding came in 1959 following a transfer from the U.S. Plant Introduction Station in Chico, California, where I had been working with tree fruits and nuts, to the Plant Introduction Station at Glenn Dale, Maryland. There, I soon became aware of a sizeable camellia collection including some 24 species, 5 related genera, and several hundred cultivar imports from Japan. In those days, the species collection alone was a rarity and a plant breeder's dream. My new position requirements involved research and administration and camellias seemed a good means to partly satisfy the former. Love and obsession of camellias was to come later. It is something that grew on me slowly, but has taken over completely even now in my retirement.

Objectives needed for breeding

One should not embark on a breeding program without one or more objectives in mind. Among the species available were:- *C. lutchuensis*, *C. tsaii*, *C. kissi*, and *C. fraterna*, with their highly fragrant but small, white, single flowers. The first challenge (objective) was to incorporate fragrance from one or more of these into flowers with commercially acceptable size and quality. As things evolved, *C. lutchuensis* proved to be much the best of the three, so the greatest efforts were concentrated on hybridizing with this species. Crosses using *C. lutchuensis* as the pollen parent were far more successful than when used as a seed parent. Much later on, a heating malfunction in the greenhouse showed that *C. lutchuensis* needs warmer temperatures (24 to 29°C) during the flowering season to reliably set seed.

Beginner's luck

A stroke of beginner's luck with the first year's crosses resulted in a *C. rusticana* x *C. lutchuensis* hybrid which was later named 'Fragrant Pink'. Although still on the small side (classified as a miniature), it is a clear, deep pink, peony form with pleasing sweet olive-like fragrance. This set the stage for expanding the program into making several thousand crosses each year. However, the task proved more formidable than first realized. All first generation (F1) hybrids were only moderately larger than *C. lutchuensis* and they were highly sterile, both as pollen and as seed parents. The next several years brought out some promising F1 hybrids, later named 'Cinnamon Cindy', 'Fragrant Joy', 'Spring Wind', and 'Fragrance of Sleeve'. Although I found these rather pleasing, because of their small size they never gained appreciable popularity in America. Yet, 'Cinnamon Cindy', seems rather popular in Australia. 'Spring Wind' and 'Fragrance of Sleeve', on the other hand, were much admired by several Japanese friends and were introduced in Japan.

Later (1982), a branch mutation developed on 'Cinnamon Cindy' to produce a rose pink to white single with high fragrance, greater than 'Cinnamon Cindy'. This was eventually named 'Cinnamon Scentsation' in 1994.

Registration

The breeding program had to advance beyond the F1 generation if further progress was to be made. Somehow, at least one F1 hybrid had to be made fertile if backcrosses were to be made, or two or more Fls made fertile to become involved in sib crosses. A literature search disclosed that sterility barriers in interspecific hybrids had been overcome in *Vitis* (grapes), *Rubus* (raspberries), *Vaccinium* (blueberries), *Fragaria* (strawberries) and several other genera by the use of colchicine-induced polyploids. An arrangement was made with Dr. Haig Dermen, research cytologist, USDA, Beltsville, MD, to conduct some cooperative experiments. 'Fragrant Pink' was selected for treatment and was successfully converted to a fertile amphidiploid (allo-tetraploid) which was named 'Fragrant Pink Improved.' The breeding program was then advanced resulting in 'Ack-Scent', a shell pink, medium, full peony form with a spicy fragrance. This was followed by a group of six in an 'Ack-Scent' series, which were registered with the USDA in 1982. However, only 'AckScent Spice', a deep rose red, medium, peony form with an even stronger spicy fragrance than 'Ack-Scent', was eventually registered with the American Camellia Society.

There is an old saying "What goes around, comes around". That which was appropriate in the late 1960s for furthering the breeding on fragrance may well apply today in breeding for yellow flower color. More about that later.

Cold Hardiness

It was in the late 1970s and early 1980s that the Washington, DC, metropolitan area experienced a series of very severe winters. The U.S. National Arboretum collection of some 950 specimens, many 30 to 40 years old, was reduced to less than a dozen salvageable plants. Floral fragrance seemed a luxury we could not afford if our camellias would not survive our winters. Thus, all new work on fragrance and work begun with *C. nitidissima* (*C. chrysantha*), was put on hold and our full efforts were given towards developing greater cold hardiness.

Among the surviving camellias at the Arboretum was a specimen of *C. oleifera*, introduced from China in 1948. It not only survived without injury, but flowered uninterrupted each autumn. *C.oleifera* is widely grown in the Orient, not as an ornamental, but as a source of seeds, which are pressed to produce cooking oils, used as a hair dressing, and in cosmetics. We secured five strains of *C. oleifera* that had been collected throughout the Orient. Of these, only one was comparable in hardiness to the Arboretum plant.

These two strains were to become the basis for over 7,000 crosses involving cultivars of *C. sasanqua*, *C. hiemalis*, *C. vernalis*, *C. japonica*, *C. rusticana*, and C X *williamsii*.

How low can you go?

This resulted in 2,500 interspecific hybrids which were greenhouse grown until 1982 and then planted out for field testing at 14 locations in Pennsylvania, Maryland, Virginia, North Carolina, and Washington, DC. Protection from the elements varied at the individual sites, ranging from an overstorey of mature pines and/or deciduous trees to lath and shade houses. Thus far, they have experienced minimum temperatures ranging from -22 to -26°C. Plants that showed little or no injury were then judged for their flower quality and overall marketability.

A series of 13 fall flowering hybrids were developed, including 'Ashton's Pride', 'Frost Princess', 'Polar Ice', 'Snow Flurry', 'Winter's Beauty', 'Winter's Charm', 'Winter's Dream', 'Winter's Hope', 'Winter's Interlude', 'Winter's Peony', 'Winter's Rose', 'Winter's Star', and 'Winter's Waterlily'. Seven spring flowering hybrids, including 'Frost Queen', 'Betty Sette', 'Fire 'n Ice', 'Ice Follies', 'Pink Icicle', 'Spring Frill' and 'Jerry Hill', were introduced, starting in 1986.

A number of these cultivars are now being successfully established in areas where camellias were not previously grown outdoors. New England has never been considered 'camellia country', yet these plants are thriving in coastal regions of Connecticut, Rhode Island, and Massachusetts. A hardy camellia is no longer a dream. Gardeners who live in areas where the winter extremes do not fall below -23°C (USDA Zone 6a), and where some protection from winter winds and early morning sun can be provided, should be encouraged to try these hybrids.

Exposure to intense sunlight

One of the overall objectives of the breeding program was to extend the culture of camellias into areas where they could be grown only with difficulty. Most of the emphasis was to extend the range northward, but camellias also did not do well in the very deep south, when exposed to intense sunlight and heat. Thus, a series of hybrids was developed and tested in the most southern parts of Florida and California. This ultimately resulted in the introduction of 'Sun Worshipper' and 'Two Marthas'.

The elusive yellow

After a lapse of more than ten years, work was begun again (in 1995) with *C. nitidissima* (*C. chrysantha*), in an effort to transfer yellow color into commercially acceptable flowers. At the present (early 1997), hybridizers throughout much of the camellia world have successfully developed a multitude of valid F1 interspecific hybrids.

Yet, I am not aware of any claims of any hybrids with yellow pigmentation comparable to *C. nitidissima*. No one seems to have advanced beyond the F1 generation because of the severe sterility among these hybrids. To adequately explore the possibilities of recessive inheritance one must advance to additional generations through sib and/or backcrosses. The problem appears almost identical with that which I faced in the late 1960s and solved through colchicine-induced polyploids.

Imagination and Patience

It is my opinion that without serious new challenges (objectives), breeding camellias will eventually stagnate and become a labor of diminishing returns. With new species coming out of China, we have a seemingly continuous supply of unique germ plasm with which to work. All it takes is imagination and patience to achieve new goals. It all makes life more interesting and worthwhile.

C. hybrid 'Ack-Scent'[7]

C. hybrid 'Fire 'n Ice'[7]

C. hybrid 'Winter's Charm'[7]

* Research Horticulturist (retired) Agricultural Research Service, USDA U.S. National Arboretum Washington, DC, U.S.A.

7 Photographs supplied by Dr William Ackerman

Preparing Camellias for Exhibition

by Hulyn Smith*

Early morning

It is really very interesting to go to a camellia show early in the morning and watch friends preparing their blossoms for display. Many of them are serious competing exhibitors while a few are preparing their blooms for display only, as I am doing now. The preparation of blooms for both types of exhibitors is similar. We strive to put the very best flowers on display—perhaps to win a trophy, sell a plant, or interest other people in our hobby.

But what about the less serious grower who just walked in with his flowers that look like ten miles of muddy roads. These poor blossoms were probably good flowers early in the morning, but somewhere between cutting and displaying, he managed to destroy his blooms. We must attempt to teach him better.

I am very serious about the flowers I display and I would like to share with you some of the things I do that I believe are important and critical for exhibitors.

Cutting blossoms

I start cutting blooms on Sunday morning in preparation for the following Saturday show. I select only blooms that are at their peak or very near their peak. I never cut a flower that is even slightly beyond its peak. My flowers are cut with a 3 to 4 inch stem and the stem is immediately placed in a glass of water. Practically all of the candidates for display had their leaves pinned back with clothes pins one to two weeks early to prevent damage in opening.

Grooming the blossoms

Now is the time to fine tune the flowers for the show. I remove all moisture from the bloom. If there is a lot of moisture, I use an 8 inch pair of industrial tweezers with cotton balls. If there is only a small amount of moisture I use a Q-tip. I am careful to also remove all pollen or any debris that is on the petals. The blossom is now ready to be sprayed with Clear Set. This product locks in moisture and makes the blossom, which is over 95% water, last longer. I spray the blossom lightly, fanning the spray can from side to side as I walk around the flower and then fan across the top. I never point the spray can directly at the blossom to start the spray action. This can cause a blob of chemical to hit and ruin the flower. I also spray the back of the bloom after I have removed the leaves, being certain to spray the calyx well. After spraying the blossom and it has thoroughly dried, I then carefully check the blossom for balance—petals that are too close to each other, large peony petals that have flopped or any situation where a cotton ball could be placed to improve the shape of the flower. Keep in mind this blossom is going to a flower show and must look its absolute best.

Spring blooms

I put all my flowers in 10-cup Tupperware containers for refrigeration storage until show day (38-40 degrees F.) Each container is lined with about a one inch "birdnest" layer of polyfil or pillow fiber. In this "birdnest" I put a bottle cap. A roll-on deodorant cap is perfect. The cap is filled with either Chrysal or Floralife, mixed according to the manufacturer's instructions. Both of these products seem to produce about the same results. Now I take the bloom and cut the stem to only one inch. I then carefully place the flower in the bottle cap in the Tupperware container lined with polyfil. The blossom is now ready for show day except for the leaf. I select the best leaf of this variety I can find and cut off $1/4$ of the stem end. After carefully cleaning this leaf I staple a 1" x 2" piece of index card to the stem end of the leaf and punch a hole in the end of the card. The leaf is now put into the container and the flower and leaf are secured so it cannot move with polyfil. The container is now sealed, put in the refrigerator and not opened again until it is time to display at the show.

Transporting flowers

Whether I leave on Friday afternoon or Saturday morning for the show, my procedure is the same. I pack my containers in boxes with frozen blue ice sufficient to keep camellias cool enough to get to the show bench. Needless to say, I drive carefully to avoid having to slam on brakes.

Staging and the show bench

Once you get to the show, the balance of the work is easy. Open your container, carefully remove the flower and leaf. The leaf is now affixed to the stem with only one inch of the leaf showing and is turned on the stem to its best position. The flower is placed in the show and now ready for display.

Everything I have told you in this article is completely legal according to ACS rules. You can probably get by with less work in preparation. However, many do much more work.

Keep in mind there is as much in showing as there is in growing.

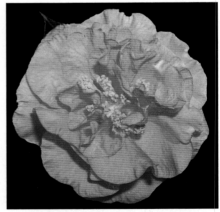

C. reticulata 'Hulyn Smith'

* 2436 Meadowbrook Drive, Valdosta, Georgia, 3162, USA

The CAMELLIA IDENTIFICATION PHOTOGRAPHIC DICTIONARY

A photo dictionary and descriptive guide
of almost 1,100 camellia plants arranged
alphabetically within each category,
with the most popular, *Camellia japonica*,
being listed first.

Camellia japonica

Of the various camellia species, *C. japonica* is the most widely grown and by far the most popular for the average gardener. This species has a very wide range of cultivars in a varying range of colours of reds, pinks, mauvish reds, creams, whites and many bi-colours.

Flower Form

The flowers encompass all of the flower forms and range of sizes. Hobbyists and exhibitors find *C. japonica* to be very popular and it is not unusual for these enthusiasts to have more that 1,000 different cultivars in their collections.

Climate

C. japonica are reasonably cold hardy. Most are able to withstand temperatures of 5° below freezing with some tolerating odd, short cold snaps to 10° below freezing, so long as these temperatures are only for a very short time. If temperatures as low as 5° below freezing are constant, premature death will probably eventuate. In the USA, zones 7-9 are regarded as the best climatic zones for *C. japonica*. For plants that fall outside of this category the notes under the relevant photograph describe their cold tolerance. Breeding programs are being undertaken to hybridize *C. japonica* with the very cold hardy Camellia species. Attempts are also being made to breed more cold tolerant *C. japonica* hybrids and reselection methods are being used to get more cold tolerant plants from existing cultivars.

Main Species

C. japonica is believed to be the main species of camellia to be cultivated as an ornamental plant in both Japan and China, about 500 years ago. In this period of time it has been estimated that more than 20,000 *C. japonica* cultivars may have been grown but many different names have been given to the same cultivar.

> *Note: Form, colour and size may vary depending on location*

New Cultivars

There are many new cultivars being introduced every year, with mutations or sports (as many people call them) being found each year. It is not uncommon for cultivars such as 'Betty Sheffied', 'Tomorrow' or 'Aspasia Macarthur' to have 3 or 4 different coloured flowers on a large plant at the same time. From my experience the older the cultivar, the more it is likely to mutate and give us a new cultivar.

The new cultivars are most likely to come from the countries with the most camellia growers such as U.S.A, the British Isles, Australia, Japan, New Zealand and China, although with China the new cultivars are more likely to be from other species.

Many *C. japonica*, especially new releases, are grafted, using one of the more vigorous *C. sasanqua* as root stock. This has the advantage of making the plant more resistant to root diseases, which occasionally cause premature death in camellias.

Site Selection

When growning japonica camellias, it is essential to select a site which has good drainage and an open, friable soil which is slightly acid. These camellias in particular can be affected by shortages of iron and magnesium if the soil is too acid. This can be easily identified by the overall yellowing of the plants leaves. Spraying with iron chelates and Epsom Salts every three months is advisable.

Site selection in the garden is also an important feature as these camellias dislike windy aspects and poor drainage.

It is preferable to grow the plants in a situation where they receive morning sun only. This aspect gives better quality flowers, of more intense colour.

Containers

Many gardeners grow their japonicas in large pots but care must be taken not to use concrete or cement pots as this can cause the soil to become too alkaline. Hot summers can have a drying effect on the pots so a good watering program is essential.

At Camellia exhibitions it is easy to see the popularity of the japonica cultivars as often they may number up to 70%

of all flowers exhibited, and often the champion of the show will come from this group.

One of the most noticeable things about *C. japonica* flowers to the average gardener is the similarity between several different cultivars, which, to the untrained eye, appear to be the same.

It is only the flower appearance which seems to be the same as many other factors need to be looked at to see the differences.

These included early, mid-season or late flowering, tall, medium, compact or spreading plants, or different leaf features such as smooth or serrated leaves. Some flowers may fade as they age whilst others hold their colour well. In one climate, one cultivar may perform better than another cultivar with a similar looking flower.

Most gardeners choosing their first camellia usually choose it from the shape and colour of the flower and if they find that selection grows and flowers well they then make a more in-depth study for their next selection.

During the years I owned a nursery I found that first selection were japonica formal doubles of pink or red which led to good sales of such cultivars as 'Prince Frederick William', 'William Bull', 'C. M. Hovey' and 'Prince Eugene Napoleon'.

These were quite hardy in my area and the new camellia growers had mostly success with their first selections. Many of these early gardeners are now camellia enthusiasts.

Over the last few years when I have spoken to nurserymen selling camellias, I have been told that formal double japonicas are usually the first selection, with the pink and white bi-colours such as 'Commander Mulroy', 'Desire', 'Grace Albritton', 'Blushing Beauty' and 'Tammia' now being popular.

The prize winning 'Tammia', which I saw in Atlanta in early 1997, was one of the most outstanding formal *C. japonicas* I have seen and is featured in the colour dictionary section of this book.

With new miniatures being more available at nurseries their popularity is growing rapidly.

C. japonica 'Adolphe Audusson'
[syn. Audrey Hopfer, Adolphe Audusson
Red, Adolphe Audusson Purple]
Semi-double, large size flower, mid-season,
large, bushy.
National Camellia Hall of Fame, 1978; RHS, FCC, 1956.

C. japonica 'Akashigata'
[syn. Lady Clare, Pink Czar, Empress,
Nellie Bly]
Semi-double, large size flower, early to mid-
season, large, bushy.
RHS Award of Merit, 1927; National Hall of Fame,
1978 as 'Lady Clare'.

C. japonica 'Alice Wood'
Formal double, large size flower, early to
mid-season, large, upright.

C. japonica 'Adolphe Audusson
                              Variegated'
[syn. Adolphe Audusson Variant, Adolphe
Audusson (Blotched)]
Semi-double, large size flower, mid-season,
large, bushy.
William E. Woodroof Hall of Fame, 1978.

C. japonica 'Alba Plena'
[syn. Nankin-shiro, Da Bai, Old White,
French White]
Formal double, medium to large size flower,
early to late season, medium, bushy.

C. japonica 'Allene Gunn'
Peony-form, medium size flower, mid-
season, medium, upright.

C. japonica 'Ai-no-yama'
Single, medium size flower, mid-season,
large, upright.

C. japonica 'Alexander Hunter'
[syn. Alex Hunter]
Single to semi-double, medium size flower,
early to mid-season, large, upright. Some
flowers may have white markings.

C. japonica 'Althaeiflora'
[syn. Childsii, Rosette, Thunbergia]
Peony-form, large size flower, mid-season,
large, spreading.
RHS Award of Merit, 1950; Award of Garden Merit,
1953.

C. japonica 'Amagashita'
Single to semi-double, medium to large size flower, mid-season, medium, spreading.

C. japonica 'Angel's Blush'
[syn. Melissa Martini]
Semi-double, miniature size flower, mid-season, medium, bushy.

C. japonica 'Ann Clayton'
Formal double, miniature size flower, late season, medium, upright.

C. japonica 'Ama-obune'
[syn. Cambridge Red, May McDonald, Mount Albert Red]
Semi-double, medium size flower, mid-season, medium, spreading.

C. japonica 'Ann Blair Brown'
Anemone, large size flower, mid-season, medium, upright.

C. japonica 'Apollo Variegated'
Semi-double, medium size flower, mid-season, medium, upright.

C. japonica 'Anemoniflora'
[syn. Waratah, Anemoniflora Waratah, Mrs Sol Runyon, Honey Comb]
Anemone, medium size flower, mid-season, medium, upright.

C. japonica 'Ann Blair Brown Variegated'
Anemone, large size flower, mid-season, medium, upright.

C. japonica 'Ardoch'
Semi-double to double, medium size flower, mid-season, medium, upright.

C. japonica 'Ariana Hall'
Semi-double, large size flower, mid to late season, medium, upright.

C. japonica 'Astronaut Variegated'
Single to semi-double, large size flower, mid-season, medium, upright. Many flowers show more white than illustration.

C. japonica 'Ave Maria'
Peony-form to formal double, small to medium size flower, early to mid-season, medium, upright, bushy.
Marbury Award, 1993; William E. Woodroof Hall of Fame, 1991.

C. japonica 'Aspasia Macarthur'
[syn. Flore Celeste, Aspasia]
Peony-form, medium size flower, mid to late season, large, bushy.

C. japonica 'Augusto Leal de Gouveia Pinto'
[syn. Jack McCaskill, Portugese Pink]
Semi-double to formal double, large size flower, mid-season, medium, upright.
William Hertrich Award as 'Jack McCaskill'; RHS Award of Merit, 1958.

C. japonica 'Awayuki'
Single to semi-double, small size flower, mid to late season, medium, upright. Relatively frost hardy to -10°.

C. japonica 'Astronaut'
Single to semi-double, large size flower, mid-season, medium, upright.

C. japonica 'Aunt Jetty'
[syn. Red Governor Mouton, Hexagonia Rubra]
Peony-form to semi-double, medium size flower, mid to late season, medium, upright.

C. japonica 'Baby Doll'
Anemone, miniature size flower, mid-season, medium, spreading.

C. japonica 'Baby Pearl'
Formal double, small size flower, mid to late season, medium, bushy. A small reflexed flower form.
William E. Wyłam Award, 1992.

C. japonica 'Bambino'
Anemone to peony form, miniature size flower, mid-season, large, bushy.

C. japonica 'Bart Colbert Variegated'
Semi-double to rose-form, large size flower, early to mid-season, medium, upright.

C. japonica 'Baby Sis'
Semi-double to anemone, small size flower, mid-season, medium, bushy.

C. japonica 'Barbara Morgan'
[syn. Nigger Red]
Semi-double to incomplete double, large size flower, mid-season, medium, bushy.

C. japonica 'Beauté de Nantes'
[syn. Rose Queen, Busch Garden Red, Beauty of Nantes, Beauty, Bush Red]
Roseform, medium to large size flower, late season, medium, bushy.

C. japonica 'Ballet Dancer'
Peony-form, medium size flower, mid-season, medium, upright.

C. japonica 'Barbara Woodroof'
Semi-double to anemone, medium to large size flower, early to mid-season, medium, spreading.

C. japonica 'Bella Lambertii'
Roseform to peony, large size flower, mid-season, medium, upright.

C. japonica 'Bella Romana Pink'
Roseform to formal double, medium to large size flower, mid-season, medium upright.

C. japonica 'Benten'
Single, small size flower, mid-season, medium, upright. A cultivar with variegated foliage.

C. japonica 'Betty Boardman Variegated'
Semi-double, medium to large size flower, mid-season, medium, bushy.

C. japonica 'Benibotan'
[syn. Batista, Harmonius, Herme Pink, Herme Red, Majestic, Hikarugenji-Aka, Pink Jordan's Pride, Powell's Pink, Radiant Glow, Rosy Dawn, Wings, Jordan's Pride Red, Red Herme] Semi-double to peony, large size flower, mid-season, large, upright.

C. japonica 'Berenice Perfection'
Formal double, medium size flower, mid-season, large, upright.

C. japonica 'Betty Cuthbert'
Informal double, large size flower, mid-season, medium, spreading.

C. japonica 'Benikarako'
[syn. Beni-bokuhan]
Anemone, small to medium size flower, mid-season, medium, upright.

C. japonica 'Bessie McArthur'
Semi-double to peony, medium to large size flower, late season, small, bushy.

C. japonica 'Betty Foy Sanders'
Semi-double, large size flower, mid-season, medium, bushy.

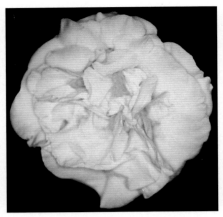

C. japonica 'Betty Sheffield'
Semi-double to peony, medium to large size flower, mid-season, medium, bushy. This Camellia has unstable flower colours and produces many sports.

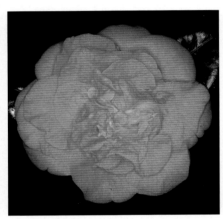

C. japonica 'Betty Sheffield Dream'
Semi-double to peony, medium to large size flower, mid-season, medium, bushy.

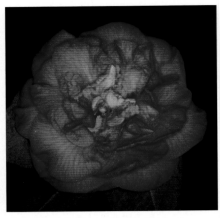

C. japonica 'Betty Sheffield Red'
Semi-double to peony, medium to large size flower, mid-season, medium, bushy.

C. japonica 'Betty Sheffield Blush Supreme'
Semi-double to peony, medium to large size flower, mid-season, medium, bushy.

C. japonica 'Betty Sheffield Pink'
Semi-double to peony, large size flower, mid-season, medium, bushy.

C. japonica 'Betty Sheffield Silver'
Semi-double to peony, medium to large size flower, mid-season, medium, bushy.

C. japonica 'Betty Sheffield Coral Variegated'
Semi-double to peony, medium to large size flower, mid-season, medium, bushy.

C. japonica 'Betty Sheffield Pink Chiffon'
Semi-double to peony, medium to large size flower, mid-season, medium, bushy.

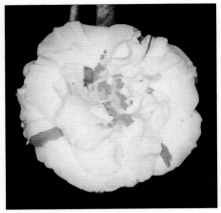

C. japonica 'Betty Sheffield Supreme'
Semi-double to peony, medium to large size flower, mid-season, medium, bushy.
William Hertrich Award, 1963.

C. japonica 'Betty Sheffield Variegated'
[syn. Betty Sheffield Pink Variegated]
Semi-double to peony, medium to large size
flower, mid-season, medium, bushy.

C. japonica 'Bicentenary Joy'
Formal double, medium to large size flower,
mid-season, medium, bushy.

C. japonica 'Black Velvet'
Formal double, large size flower,
mid-season, medium, upright.

C. japonica 'Betty Sheffield White'
Semi-double to peony, medium to large size
flower, mid to late season, medium,
bushy.

C. japonica 'Black Magic'
Semi-double to roseform, medium size
flower, mid to late season, medium,
spreading. Has leaves like Holly leaves.

C. japonica 'Blaze of Glory'
Semi-double to peony to anemone, large size
flower, early to mid-season, medium,
upright.

C. japonica 'Betty's Beauty'
[syn. Rudy Moore]
Semi-double to peony, medium to large size
flower, mid-season, medium, bushy.
William Hertrich Award, 1987.

C. japonica 'Black Tie'
Formal double, small size flower,
mid-season, medium, upright.
William E. Wylan Award, 1990.

C. japonica 'Blood of China'
[syn. Alice Slack, Victor Emanuel]
Peony-form, large size flower, mid to late
season, medium, bushy.

C. japonica 'Blushing Beauty'
Formal double, medium size flower, mid-season, medium, upright.

C. japonica 'Bokuhan'
[syn. Tinsie, Gakkô, Gekkô, Bokuhan-tsubaki]
Anemone, miniature size flower, mid-season, medium, upright.

C. japonica 'Burgundy Gem'
Anemone to peony form, miniature size flower, mid-season, medium, upright.

C. japonica 'Bob Hope'
Semi-double, large size flower, mid to late season, medium, bushy and upright.

C. japonica 'Brushfield's Yellow'
Anemone, medium size flower, mid-season, medium, upright.

C. japonica 'Burnham Beeches'
Informal double to peony-form, large size flower, mid-season, medium, upright.

C. japonica 'Bob's Tinsie'
Anemone, miniature to small size flower, mid-season, medium, upright.
William E. Wylan Award, 1987.

C. japonica 'Buddy Variegated'
Semi-double, small size flower, mid-season, small, bushy, perfumed.

C. japonica 'C. M. Hovey'
[syn. Colonel Firey, Firey King, William S. Hastie, Mississippi Hastie, Solaris, Duc de Devonshire]
Formal double, large size flower, late season, large, upright.
First Class Certificate RHS, 1879.

C. japonica 'C. M. Wilson'
[syn. Grace Burkhard, Lucille Ferrell]
Anemone, large size flower, early to mid-season, medium, bushy.
RHS Award of Merit, 1956.

C. japonica 'Can Can'
[syn. Kenken]
Peony-form, medium to large size flower, mid to late season, medium, bushy.

C. japonica 'Cara Mia'
Semi-double, large size flower, early to mid-season, medium, upright.

C. japonica 'Cameo Gem'
Peony-form, small size flower, mid to late season, medium, upright.

C. japonica 'Candy Apple'
Semi-double to peony, medium to large size flower, mid-season, medium, upright.

C. japonica 'Cardinal's Cap'
Anemone, small size flower, mid-season, medium, upright.

C. japonica 'Campari'
Formal double, medium to large size flower, mid-season, medium, upright.

C. japonica 'Canterbury'
Semi-double to peony, medium to large size flower, mid-season, medium, upright.

C. japonica 'Carolyn Tuttle'
Peony-form, medium to large size flower, early to late season, medium, bushy and upright.

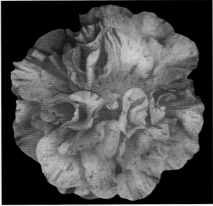

C. japonica 'Carter's Sunburst'
Semi-double to peony to formal double, large size flower, mid to late season, medium, spreading.
National Camellia Hall of Fame, 1978; Margarete Hertrich Award, 1963; John Illges Award, 1964; RHS Award of Merit, 1977.

C. japonica 'Celeste G.'
Semi-double, large size flower, mid-season, medium, upright.

C. japonica 'Cherries Jubilee'
Semi-double to rose-form, medium to large size flower, mid-season, medium, bushy and upright.
Margerete Hertrich Award, 1991.

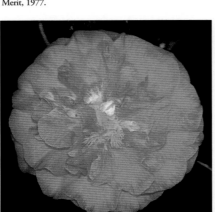

C. japonica 'Carter's Sunburst Pink'
Semi-double to peony to formal double, large size flower, mid to late season, medium, spreading.
Sewell Mutant Award, 1968; William Hertrich Award, 1970; RHS Award of Merit, 1977.

C. japonica 'Chandler's Victory'
Peony-form, large size flower, mid-season, medium, upright.

C. japonica 'China Doll'
Peony-form, large size flower, mid-season, medium, bushy.

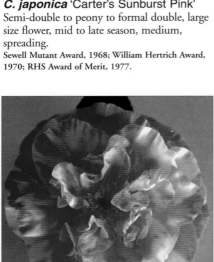

C. japonica 'Carter's Sunburst Pink Variegated'
Semi-double to peony to formal double, large size flower, mid to late season, medium, spreading.

C. japonica 'Charlie Bettes'
Semi-double, large size flower, early season, medium, bushy.

C. japonica 'Chô-chô-san'
[syn. Madame Butterfly, Palmerston, Qiaosang]
Semi-double to anemone, large size flower, mid-season, medium, bushy.

C. japonica 'Cinderella'
[syn. Huiguniang]
Semi-double, medium size flower, mid-season, medium, upright. There are two forms of Cinderella grown. One with a smooth edge, and one with a fimbriated edge as registered.

C. japonica 'Claudia Phelps'[1]
[syn. Coral Duchess, Tillie Rice]
Semi-double, large size flower, mid-season, medium, spreading.

C. japonica 'Cliff Harris'
Semi-double to peony, medium to large size flower, mid-season, medium, bushy.

C. japonica 'Clara Brooks'[1]
Semi-double to anemone, medium size flower, mid-season, medium, upright.

C. japonica 'Cleve James'
Semi-double to peony to rose form, very large size flower, mid-season, medium, bushy.

C. japonica 'Commander Mulroy'
[syn. Monuoyi Shangxiao]
Formal double, medium size flower, mid-season, medium, bushy.

C. japonica 'Clarise Carleton'
Semi-double, large size flower, mid-season, medium, upright.

C. japonica 'Cleve James Variegated'
Semi-double to peony to rose form, very large size flower, mid-season, medium, bushy.

C. japonica 'Confetti Blush'
Anemone to formal double, small to minature size flower, mid-season, medium, bushy and upright.

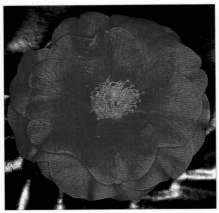

C. japonica 'Constancy'
Semi-double to peony, medium size flower,
mid-season, medium, upright.

C. japonica 'Coronation'
Semi-double, very large size flower, mid-
season, medium, spreading.
Margerete Hertrich Award, 1976; William Woodroof
Camellia Hall of Fame, 1979.

C. japonica 'Cover Girl'
Formal double, medium size flower, mid to
late season, medium, bushy.

C. japonica 'Coquettii'
[syn. Glen 40, Coquettii Vera, Alabama]
Formal double to rose-form, large size
flower, mid to late season, medium,
compact.
RHS Award of Merit, 1956.

C. japonica 'Cotton Tail'
Peony-form, miniature size flower, mid-
season, upright compact.
William E. Wylan Award, 1981.

C. japonica 'Dahlohnega'
[syn. Nuccio's Golden Anniversary]
Formal double, small size flower, mid-season,
medium, upright.

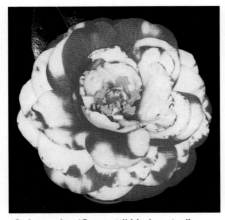

C. japonica 'Coquettii Variegated'
Roseform to formal double, medium to
large size flower, mid to late season,
medium, bushy and upright.

C. japonica 'Countess of Orkney Rosea'
Peony-form, large size flower, mid-season,
medium, upright.

C. japonica 'Daikagura'[1]
[syn. Shôjitsu, Kiyosu, Daikagura Variegated,
Seihi, Lion's Dance, Shônichi, Shôhi, Teruhi]
Peony-form, large size flower, early season,
medium, upright.

C. japonica 'Dainty Maiden'
Semi-double to informal double, medium to large size flower, mid to late season, pendulous growth.
RHS Preliminary Commendation, 1967.

C. japonica 'Debutante'
[syn. Sarah C. Hastie]
Peony-form, medium size flower, early to mid-season, medium, bushy and upright.

C. japonica 'Demi-Tasse'
Semi-double, miniature to small size flower, mid-season, bushy, compact.
William E. Wylam 'Miniature Award', 1971.

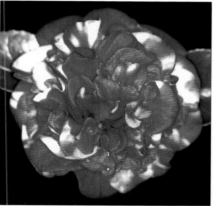

C. japonica 'Dark of the Moon Variegated'
Peony-form, large size flower, mid-season, medium, bushy and upright.

C. japonica 'Dee Davis'
Rose-form, medium size flower, mid-season, medium, upright and open.

C. japonica 'Desire'
Formal double, medium size flower, mid-season, medium, bushy and upright.

C. japonica 'Dawn's Early Light'
Peony-form, medium to large size flower, early to late season, medium, upright.

C. japonica 'Dee Davis Variegated'
Rose-form, medium size flower, early to mid-season, small, upright and open.

C. japonica 'Destiny'
Semi-double, medium to large size flower, early to mid-season, medium, bushy.

C. japonica 'Devonia'
[syn. Swan]
Single, medium to large size flower, mid-season, medium, upright.
RHS Award of Merit, 1900.

C. japonica 'Dixie Knight Supreme'
Semi-double to peony, medium to large size flower, mid to late season, medium, bushy.
William E. Woodroof Camellia Hall of Fame, 1988.

C. japonica 'Don-Mac'
Semi-double to peony, very large size flower, mid to late season, medium, upright.

C. japonica 'Diddy's Pink Organdie'
Formal double, medium size flower, mid-season, medium, slightly pendulous.

C. japonica 'Dixie Knight Variegated'
Semi-double to peony, medium to large size flower, mid to late season, medium, bushy.

C. japonica 'Dona Herzilia De Freitas Magalhaes'
Semi-double to anemone, medium size flower, mid-season, medium, upright.

C. japonica 'Dixie Knight'
Semi-double, medium to large size flower, mid to late season, medium, bushy.

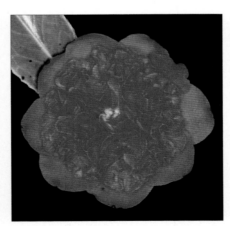

C. japonica 'Dolly Dyer'
Anemone to informal double, miniature size flower, early to mid-season, medium, upright.

C. japonica 'Donnan's Dream'
Formal double, medium to large size flower, early to late season, medium, upright.

C. japonica 'Doris Ellis'
Formal double, medium size flower, early season, medium, upright.

C. japonica 'Dr Henry B. Harvey'
Formal double, small size flower, early to mid-season, medium, bushy and upright.

C. japonica 'Dr W. G. Lee'
Semi-double, medium size flower, mid to late season, medium, bushy.

C. japonica 'Doris Freeman'[5]
Semi-double to peony, medium to large size flower, mid-season, upright, compact.

C. japonica 'Dr King'
Semi-double, large size flower, mid to late season, medium, bushy.

C. japonica 'Drama Girl'
Semi-double, very large size flower, mid-season, open pendulous growth.
National Hall of Fame Award, 1978; RHS, FCC, 1969.

C. japonica 'Dr Burnside'
Semi-double to peony, large size flower, mid-season, medium, upright.

C. japonica 'Dr Tinsley'
[syn. Tinsley]
Semi-double to double, medium size flower, mid-season, medium, bushy and upright.

C. japonica 'Easter Morn'
Semi-double to peony, large size flower, mid to late season, medium, upright.
Margarete Hertrich Award, 1971.

C. japonica 'Ecclefield'
Semi-double to anemone, very large size flower, mid-season, medium, upright.

C. japonica 'Edith Linton'
[syn. Jean Lynn Pink]
Semi-double, medium size flower, mid-season, medium, bushy.

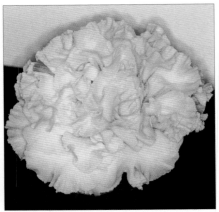

C. japonica 'Elaine Betty'
Peony-form, large size flower, mid-season, medium, upright.

C. japonica 'Ed Combatalade'
Formal double, medium size flower, mid to late season, medium, bushy.

C. japonica 'Edna Bass Variegated'[5]
Semi-double to peony, very large size flower, early season, medium, upright.

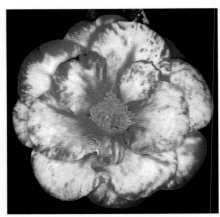

C. japonica 'Eleanor Martin Supreme'
Semi-double, large size flower, mid to late season, upright, open.
Margerete Hertrich Award, 1985.

C. japonica 'Edelweiss'
Semi-double to peony, very large size flower, early to late season, medium, weeping.
RHS Award of Merit, 1967.

C. japonica 'Edna Deadwyler'
Anemone, large size flower, mid-season, medium, spreading.

C. japonica 'Eleanor Martin Variegated'
Semi-double, large size flower, mid to late season, open, upright.

C. japonica 'Elegans'
[syn. Francine, Chandleri Elegans Pink]
Anemone, large size flower, early to mid-season, medium, spreading.

C. japonica 'Elegans Supreme'
Anemone, large size flower, early to mid-season, medium, spreading. This flower has serrated petals.
William Hertrich Award, 1967; William E. Woodroof Camellia Hall of Fame Award, 1980.

C. japonica 'Elizabeth Boardman'
Semi-double, large size flower, mid-season, medium, upright.

C. japonica 'Elegans Champagne'
Anemone, large size flower, early to mid-season, medium, spreading.
William Hertrich Award 1982; Sewell Mutant Award, 1980.

C. japonica 'Elegans Supreme Variegated'
Anemone, large size flower, early to mid-season, medium, spreading. This flower has serrated petals.

C. japonica 'Elizabeth Dowd'
Rose-form, large size flower, mid-season, medium, upright.

C. japonica 'Elegans Splendor'
Anemone, large size flower, early to mid-season, medium, spreading.
William Hertrich Award, 1972; Sewell Mutant Award, 1974.

C. japonica 'Elegans Variegated'
Anemone, large size flower, early to mid-season, medium, spreading.

C. japonica 'Elizabeth Dowd Silver'
Rose-form, large size flower, mid-season, medium, upright.
William Hertrich Award, 1986.

C. japonica 'Elizabeth Weaver'
Formal double, large size flower, early to
mid-season, upright, open.
Margerete Hertrich Award, 1992.

C. japonica 'Emmet Pfingstl'
[syn. Dorothy Parker, Joseph Pfingstl
Variegated]
Incomplete double, large size flower, mid-
season, medium, upright.

C. japonica 'Emperor of Russia
                                    Variegated'
[syn. Czarina]
Peony-form, medium to large size flower,
mid-season, medium, bushy.

C. japonica 'Elsie M. Rollinson'
Formal double, very large size flower, early
to late season, medium, upright.

C. japonica 'Emmy Roos'[1]
Peony-form, large size flower, mid to late
season, medium, upright.

C. japonica 'Erin Farmer'
Semi-double to peony, large size flower,
mid-season, medium, upright.

C. japonica 'Emmalene Variegated'
Semi-double, large size flower, early to mid-
season, medium, upright.

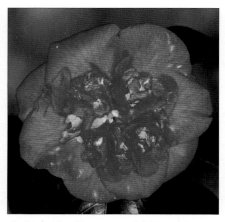

C. japonica 'Emperor of Russia'
[syn. Stevens]
Peony-form, medium to large size flower,
mid-season, medium, bushy.

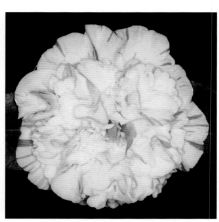

C. japonica 'Esther Smith'
Peony-form, medium size flower, mid-
season, medium, upright.

C. japonica 'Ethyl Rhyne'
Formal double, medium size flower, mid to late season, medium, upright.

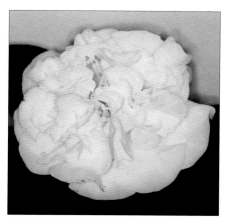

C. japonica 'Evelyn Poe'
Peony-form, medium to large size flower, mid-season, medium, spreading.

C. japonica 'Extravaganza'
[syn. Extravaganza Striped]
Anemone, very large size flower, mid-season, medium, upright.

C. japonica 'Eugene Lizé'
[syn. Lady Jane Grey, Donkelaari Eugene Lizé, Annie McDonald, Archie McDonald, Eryldene Number 1]
Semi-double to peony-form, medium to large size flower, early to mid-season, medium, upright.

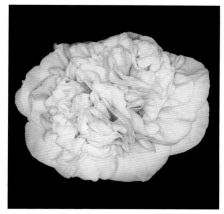

C. japonica 'Evelyn Poe Blush'
Peony-form, medium to large size flower, mid-season, medium, spreading.

C. japonica 'Faith'
Semi-double, large size flower, early to mid-season, medium, upright.

C. japonica 'Evangelia Kalafatas'
Peony-form to formal double, large size flower, early to mid-season, medium, upright.

C. japonica 'Evelyn Poe Pink'
Peony-form, medium to large size flower, mid-season, medium, spreading.

C. japonica 'Fancy Free'
Semi-double to rose-form, large size flower, mid-season, upright, compact.

C. japonica 'Fannie Loughridge
Variegated'
Anemone to peony form, large size flower,
mid-season, medium, upright.

C. japonica 'Feathery Touch'
[syn. Changyumoi]
Semi-double, medium size flower, mid-
season, medium, spreading.

C. japonica 'Finlandia Red'
[syn. Finlandia Rosea, Aurora Rosea, Pert,
Margaret Jack]
Semi-double, medium size flower, early to
mid-season, medium, bushy.

C. japonica 'Fashionata'
Semi-double, large size flower, mid-season,
medium, upright.
William E. Woodroof Camellia Hall of Fame Award, 1982.

C. japonica 'Ferol Zerkowsky'
Peony-form to semi-double, large size
flower, mid to late season, medium,
spreading.

C. japonica 'Fir Cone'
Semi-double, miniature size flower, mid-
season, medium, bushy. Mostly semi-double
in Australia and New Zealand, often rose-
form in U.S.A.
John A. Taylor Jnr Miniature Award, 1982.

C. japonica 'Fashionata Variegated'
Semi-double, large size flower, mid-season,
medium, upright.

C. japonica 'Fimbriata'
[syn. Alba Fimbriata, Fimbriata Alba]
Formal double, medium to large size flower,
early to late season, medium, upright.
Lightly serrated petals.

C. japonica 'Fir Cone Variegated'[5]
Semi-double, miniature size flower, mid-
season, medium, bushy.

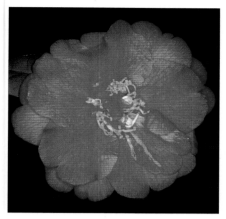

C. japonica 'Firebrand'
Semi-double, medium size flower, mid-season, medium, upright.

C. japonica 'First Prom'
Formal double, medium size flower, early to late season, medium, bushy and upright.

C. japonica 'Flowerwood'
[syn. Mathotiana Fimbriata]
Rose-form to peony, large size flower, mid to late season, medium, upright. The outer petals are lightly serrated.

C. japonica 'Fire Dance'
Semi-double, medium size flower, mid-season, medium, bushy and upright.

C. japonica 'Flamingo'
Semi-double, medium size flower, early season, medium, upright.

C. japonica 'Fortune Teller'
Peony-form, large size flower, mid to late season, medium, bushy.

C. japonica 'Fire Falls'
Double, medium to large size flower, early to late season, medium, upright.

C. japonica 'Fleur Dipater'
[syn. Fleur De Pêche, Peach Blossom]
Semi-double, medium size flower, mid-season, medium, upright.

C. japonica 'Fran Homeyer'
Formal double, medium to large size flower, early to mid-season, medium, spreading.

C. japonica 'Fran Mathis'
Semi-double, medium to large size flower,
early to mid-season, medium, upright.

C. japonica 'Frau Geheimrat Oldevig'
[syn. Mme Chiang Kai-Shek, Thomas Plant]
Semi-double, medium size flower, mid-
season, medium, bushy.

C. japonica 'Funny Face Betty'
[syn. Charming Betty, Charming Betty
Sheffield]
Peony-form to semi-double, medium to
large size flower, mid-season, medium,
bushy.

C. japonica 'Frances Butler'
Semi-double, medium size flower, mid-
season, medium, bushy.

C. japonica 'Frost Queen'[7]
Semi-double, large size flower, early to late
season, medium, upright, cold hardy.

C. japonica 'Furô-An'
Single, medium size flower, mid-season,
medium, upright.
Award of Merit RHS, 1956.

C. japonica 'Frances Hill'
Informal to semi-double, large size flower,
mid-season, medium, upright.

C. japonica 'Frosty Morn'
Anemone to peony form, large size flower,
mid to late season, medium, open growth.

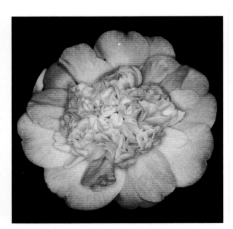

C. japonica 'Gayle Walden'
Anemone to peony form, medium to large
size flower, mid-season, medium, upright.

C. japonica 'Gee Homeyer'[1]
Formal double, medium size flower, mid-season, medium, upright.

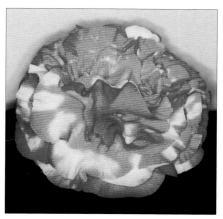

C. japonica 'Georgia National Fair'
Semi-double to peony, very large size flower, early to late season, medium, upright.

C. japonica 'Glacier'
Semi-double, medium to large size flower, mid-season, medium, upright.

C. japonica 'General Leclerc'
Semi-double to peony, large size flower, mid-season, medium, compact.

C. japonica 'Georgia Rouse'
Peony-form, medium to large size flower, early to mid-season, medium, bushy and spreading.

C. japonica 'Gladys Pinkerton'
Peony-form to semi-double, large size flower, mid-season, medium, upright, open.

C. japonica 'Geoff Hamilton'
Formal double, medium size flower, mid to late season, medium, bushy and spreading. Grown mostly for its showy variegated foliage.

C. japonica 'Gigantea'
[syn. Kelvingtoniana, Emperor Frederick Wilhelm, Jolly Roger Gaiety, Fanny Davenport, Mary Bell Glennan, Magnolia King]
Semi-double to rose-form to peony, very large size flower, mid-season, medium, open upright.

C. japonica 'Glenn-Ella'
Peony-form, medium to large size flower, early to late season, medium, upright, slightly pendulous.

C. japonica 'Goshikichiri-tsubaki'
Semi-double, medium to large size flower, late season, medium, upright.

C. japonica 'Grace Albritton'
Formal double, small size flower, mid-season, medium, upright.
National Camellia Hall of Fame Award ,1980; William E. Wylam Miniature Award, 1979; John Illges Award, 1978.

C. japonica 'Grand Prix'
Semi-double, very large size flower, mid-season, medium, bushy and upright.
William E. Woodroof Camellia Hall of Fame Award, 1978.

C. japonica 'Governor Earl Warren'
Incomplete double, medium to large size flower, mid-season, medium, upright.

C. japonica 'Granada'
Peony-form to semi-double, large size flower, mid-season, medium, upright.

C. japonica 'Grand Slam'
Semi-double to anemone, very large size flower, mid-season, medium, upright.
RHS Award of Merit, 1975.

C. japonica 'Governor Mouton'
[syn. Governor Mouton Variegated, Variegated Governor]
Peony-form to semi-double, large size flower, mid-season, medium, spreading. Often confused with 'Aunt Jetty' which is plain red.

C. japonica 'Grand Marshall'
Anemone to peony form, medium to large size flower, mid-season, medium, upright.

C. japonica 'Grand Sultan'
[syn. Gran Sultano, Te Deum, Reticulatiflora, Midsummer's Day]
Semi-double to formal double, large size flower, mid to late season, medium, upright.

C. japonica 'Great Eastern'
[syn. Great Eastern (Australian)]
Semi-double, medium to large size flower, mid-season, medium, bushy, upright.

C. japonica 'Guilio Nuccio'
Semi-double, large to very large size flower, mid-season, medium, upright. Flowers of the Guilio Nuccio group are very variable.
Margerete Hertrich Award, 1956; John Illges Award, 1958; National Hall of Fame Award, 1978; William E. Woodroof Camellia Hall of Fame, 1978.

C. japonica 'Gwenneth Morey'
Anemone, medium size flower, mid to late season, medium, upright.

C. japonica 'Greensboro Red'
Semi-double, medium size flower, late season, bushy, compact.

C. japonica 'Guilio Nuccio Fimbriated'[1]
Semi-double, large to very large size flower, mid-season, medium, upright, petals are fimbriated.

C. japonica 'Hagoromo'
[syn. Rose of Dawn, Cho-No-Hagasane, Magnoliaeflora]
Semi-double, medium size flower, mid-season, medium, bushy.

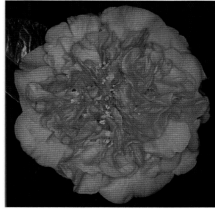

C. japonica 'Guest of Honor'
[syn. Zhubin]
Semi-double to peony, large to very large size flower, mid-season, bushy and upright, compact.
Received RHS Award of Merit, 1967.

C. japonica 'Guilio Nuccio Variegated'
Semi-double, large to very large size flower, mid-season, medium, upright.

C. japonica 'Hakuhan-kujaku'
Semi-double, small size flower, mid-season, medium, bushy.

C. japonica 'Hanafûki'
[syn. Chalice, Mrs Howard Asper]
Semi-double, medium to large size flower,
mid-season, bushy, compact.
RHS Award of Merit, 1956.

C. japonica 'Hanatachibana'
[syn. Gay Boy, Deacon Dodd, Lady Marion
Variegated]
Peony-form to rose-form, medium to large
size flower, mid to late season, medium,
upright. Flower sometimes has white
markings.

C. japonica 'Harry Cave'
Semi-double, medium size flower, early to
mid-season, medium, bushy.

C. japonica 'Hanagôri'
Semi-double, medium size flower, early to
mid-season, medium, upright.

C. japonica 'Happy Holidays'
Formal double, medium to large size flower,
early to mid-season, medium, bushy and
upright.

C. japonica 'Hawaii'
This flower has fimbriated petals, peony-
form, large size flower, early to mid-season,
medium, upright.

C. japonica 'Hana-no-sato'
Semi-double to double, large size flower,
mid-season, medium, upright.

C. japonica 'Harriet Durrant'
Peony-form to semi-double, large size
flower, mid-season, medium, spreading.

C. japonica 'Helen Boehm'
Anemone to peony form, large size flower,
mid-season, medium, upright.

C. japonica 'Helen Bower'
Rose-form, large size flower, mid to late season, medium, upright.
Sewell Mutant Award, 1971.

C. japonica 'Henry Lunsford Variegated'[5]
Peony-form to semi-double, very large size flower, mid to late season, medium, upright.

C. japonica 'High Jinks'
Rose-form to formal double, medium to large size flower, mid-season, medium, upright.

C. japonica 'Helen Bower Variegated'
Rose-form, large size flower, mid to late season, medium, upright. This picture shows only moderate white marks but often many white marks are noticeable.

C. japonica 'Her Majesty Queen Elizabeth II'
Peony-form to semi-double, medium to large size flower, mid-season, medium, upright.

C. japonica 'High Wide 'n Handsome'
Semi-double, large size flower, mid-season, medium, upright.

C. japonica 'Helenor'[6]
[syn. Guilfolius Halleana, Guilfoyle's Helena]
Rose-form, medium size flower, mid-season, large, upright.

C. japonica 'High Hat'
[syn. Pink Daikagura, Pink Kagura]
Double to peony, medium to large size flower, mid-season, upright, compact.

C. japonica 'Hikarugengi'
[syn. Herme, Jordan's Pride, Souvenir de Henri Guichard]
Semi-double to peony, medium to large size flower, mid-season, large, upright.

C. japonica 'Hilda Jamieson'
[syn. Xierda]
Semi-double, large size flower, mid to late season, medium, upright.

C. japonica 'Hollis C. Boardman'
Semi-double, medium to large size flower, mid-season, medium, upright.

C. japonica 'Hôsen'
Single, medium size flower, mid to late season, large, upright.

C. japonica 'Hishikaraito'
[syn. Emily Brown, Pink Lace, Lacy Pink]
Semi-double, small size flower, mid to late season, medium, upright.

C. japonica 'Holly Bright'
Semi-double, large size flower, mid-season, medium, bushy. This plant has unusual holly type foliage.

C. japonica 'Hototogisu'
Semi-double, medium to large size flower, mid to late season, large, upright. There appear to be at least 3 different Camellias with this name. This cultivar is grown in Kyoto Japan.

C. japonica 'Hit Parade'
Semi-double, very large size flower, mid-season, medium, upright.

C. japonica 'Honey Bee'
Formal double to peony, medium size flower, mid to late season, medium, upright. These flowers may be plain red, or red and white.

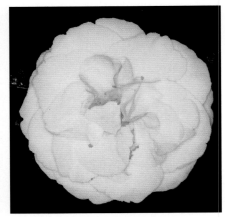

C. japonica 'Iced Fragrance'
Semi-double to peony, large size flower, early to late season, medium, upright. Fragrant flowers.

C. japonica 'Ilam Satin'
Anemone to peony form, large size flower, mid-season, medium, bushy.

C. japonica 'Imura'[1]
[syn. Imura White, Diana, Dr Allen Ames, S. Imura]
Semi-double, large size flower, mid-season, medium, upright.

C. japonica 'Iwane-shibori'
[syn. Denny D. Sport, Sunrise]
Semi-double, medium to large size flower, mid-season, large, upright. One of the most popular camellias in Japan.

C. japonica 'Imperator'
[syn. Corrie Belle, Big Daddy]
Peony-form, medium size flower, early season, medium, bushy.
Note: This should not be confused with two other Camellias of the same name.

C. japonica 'Island of Fire'
Semi-double, large size flower, mid-season, medium, upright.

C. japonica 'Iyo-Fukumusume'
Semi-double, medium to large size flower, mid-season, large, upright.

C. japonica 'Imperial Splendour'
[syn. Diguo Zhihui]
Semi-double to peony, large size flower, mid to late season, medium, spreading.

C. japonica 'Ivory Tower'
Formal double, large size flower, mid-season, medium, bushy.

C. japonica 'James Allan'
Single to double (variable), large size flower, mid-season, medium, upright.

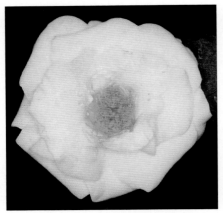

C. japonica 'Janet Waterhouse'
Semi-double, large size flower, mid-season, large, upright.

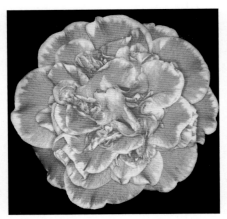

C. japonica 'Jean Clere'
Peony-form, medium to large size flower, mid to late season, large, bushy.

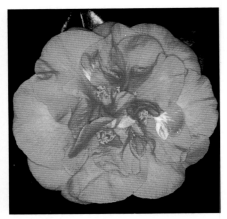

C. japonica 'Jeffrey Hood'
Semi-double to anemone, large to very large size flower, early to mid-season, large, upright.

C. japonica 'Jarvis Red'
Semi-double to peony, small to medium size flower, mid-season, medium, spreading.

C. japonica 'Jean Lyne'[6]
Semi-double to peony, medium size flower, mid-season, medium, bushy.

C. japonica 'Jerry Donnan'
Formal double, medium to large size flower, early to late season, medium, bushy. Flower has attractive "feathery" petals.

C. japonica 'Jarvis Red Variegated'
Peony-form to semi-double, small to medium size flower, mid-season, medium, spreading.

C. japonica 'Jeanette Cousins'
Semi-double, large to very large size flower, mid-season, medium, upright.

C. japonica 'Jessie Burgess'
Semi-double, large size flower, early season, medium, upright.

C. japonica 'Jessie Conner'
Formal double, small to medium size flower, mid-season, medium, upright.

C. japonica 'Joe Pyron Variegated'
Semi-double, large size flower, mid-season, upright, compact.

C. japonica 'Julia Wilson'
Semi-double, medium to large size flower, mid-season, medium, upright.

C. japonica 'Jessie Katz'
Semi-double, large size flower, mid-season, medium, upright.

C. japonica 'Jouvan'
Formal double, medium to large size flower, mid-season, medium, upright.

C. japonica 'June Holdship'
Semi-double, large size flower, mid-season, medium, upright.

C. japonica 'Jingle Bells'
Anemone, small size flower, early to mid-season, medium, upright.

C. japonica 'Julia France'
Semi-double to formal double, large size flower, mid-season, large, upright.
John Illges Award, 1972.

C. japonica 'Jupiter (Paul)'
[syn. Pauls Jupiter]
Single to semi-double, medium to large size flower, mid-season, medium, bushy and upright.
RHS Award, 1953 when exhibited as 'Apollo'.

C. japonica 'Juraku'
Single, large size flower, late season,
medium, upright.

C. japonica 'Kagoshima'
[syn. Pine Cone, Kagoshima-tsubaki,
Matsukasa-shibori]
Rose-form, medium size flower, mid to late
season, medium, upright.

C. japonica 'Karasade'
Single, medium to large size flower, early
season, medium, upright.

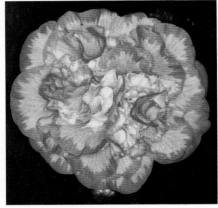

C. japonica 'Just Sue'
[syn. Maureen Ostler]
Peony-form, medium size flower, mid to late
season, bushy and upright.

C. japonica 'Kamo-honnami'
[syn. Sotan, White Swan, Yoibijin Alba,
Amabilis]
Single, large size flower, early to late season,
large, upright.

C. japonica 'Karen Henson'
Formal double, small size flower, mid-
season, medium, bushy.

C. japonica 'K. Sawada'
[syn. Silver Moon, Mrs Albert Dekker]
Rose-form to formal double, large size
flower, mid-season, medium, bushy.

C. japonica 'Kankô'
Semi-double, large size flower, mid-season,
medium, upright.

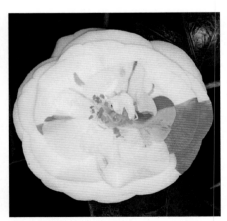

C. japonica 'Kariginu'
Semi-double to peony, medium to large size
flower, mid-season, medium, upright.

C. japonica 'Kasenzan'
[syn. Fumaiko]
Single, small size flower, mid to late season,
medium, bushy.

C. japonica 'Katie'
Semi-double, very large size flower, early to
mid-season, medium, bushy.
Margarete Hertrich Award, 1983.

C. japonica 'Kewpie Doll'
Anemone, miniature size flower, mid-season,
medium, upright.

C. japonica 'Katherine Nuccio'
Formal double to rose form, medium size
flower, mid-season, medium, bushy.

C. japonica 'Katie Variegated'
Semi-double, very large size flower, early to
mid-season, medium, bushy.

C. japonica 'Kick-Off'
Peony-form, large to very large size flower,
early to mid-season, medium, vigorous,
upright, compact.

C. japonica 'Kathryn Funari'
Formal double, large size flower, early
season, medium, upright.

C. japonica 'Kenny'
[syn. Kenny Glen]
Semi-double to peony-form, large size
flower, mid-season, medium, bushy.

C. japonica 'Kikutôji'
[syn. Chrysanthemum Season, Winter
Chrysanthemums]
Formal double, small to medium size flower,
early to mid-season, medium, upright.

C. japonica 'Kim McGowan'
Rose-form to formal double, large size
flower, mid-season, medium, bushy and
upright.

C. japonica 'Kitty'
Formal double, miniature to small size
flower, late season, medium, bushy.

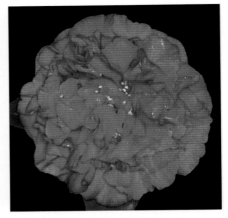

C. japonica 'Kramer's Supreme'
Peony-form, medium to large size flower, mid-
season, medium, bushy and upright, perfumed
flowers.
Frank Williams Award, 1958; William E. Woodroof
Camellia Hall of Fame Award, 1978, Margarete Hertrich
Award, 1958.

C. japonica 'King's Ransom'
Peony-form, medium size flower, mid-
season, medium, upright.

C. japonica 'Kokuryû'
[syn. Black Dragon, Carol Compton]
Semi-double to anemone, medium size
flower, mid-season, medium, upright.

C. japonica 'Kujaku'
[syn. Peacock Camellia, Benikujaku]
Single to semi-double, small size flower,
mid-season, medium, upright.

C. japonica 'Kingyo-tsubaki'
[syn. Quercifolia, Trifida, Fishtail]
Single, medium to large size flower, mid-
season, medium, upright. A compact grower
with unusual oak-like leaves. There are other
camellias named Kingyo-tsubaki which vary
from this form.

C. japonica 'Kramer's Beauty'
Peony-form, medium to large size flower,
mid-season, medium, bushy and upright,
perfumed flowers.

C. japonica 'Kuro-tsubaki'
[syn. Black Prince, Black Jap, Purpurea, Old
Port, Black Camellia]
Peony-form to semi-double, small to medium
size flower, late season, medium, bushy and
upright. Generally known as the 'Black
Camellia'.

C. japonica 'Kuroyuri'
Single, small to medium size flower, mid-season, medium, upright. Similar type of flower to 'Kujaku' but with less petals.

C. japonica 'Lady Campbell'
Rose-form, medium size flower, mid-season, medium, bushy and upright.

C. japonica 'Lady Laura'
Rose-form to formal double to peony form, large size flower, mid-season, medium, upright, The form of this flower is very variable.

C. japonica 'Kyufun-cha'
Formal double, medium size flower, mid-season, medium, upright. This is a very old Camellia and was thought to be extinct.

C. japonica 'Lady in Pink'
Semi-double, large size flower, early to mid-season, medium, upright.

C. japonica 'Lady Laura Red'
Rose-form to formal double to peony form, large size flower, mid-season, medium, upright.

C. japonica 'La Peppermint'
[syn. Brilliant Variegated]
Rose-form, medium size flower, mid-season, medium, upright.

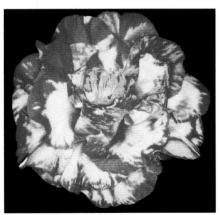

C. japonica 'Lady Kay'
[syn. Lady Kay (Lewis), Lady Kay (Bush)]
Peony-form, medium to large size flower, mid to late season, medium, upright. This flower at times has fimbriated petals.
William Hertrich Award, 1951, Sewell Mutant Award, 1983.

C. japonica 'Lady Loch'
[syn. Pink Lady, Edward Billing, Duchess of York, Elizabeth Johnston, Elizabeth of Glamis, Luochi Nushi]
Peony-form, medium to large size flower, mid to late season, medium, bushy.

C. japonica 'Lady Mary Cromartie'
[syn. Lady Mary Cromartie Pink]
Rose-form to semi-double, large size flower, mid-season, medium, upright.

C. japonica 'Lady Vansittart'
[syn. Lady Vansittart Variegated, Edo-nishiki]
Semi-double, medium size flower, mid-season, medium, bushy.

C. japonica 'Lamar Wilkes'
Peony-form, large size flower, early to late-season, medium, upright.

C. japonica 'Lady Maude Walpole'
[syn. Virginia Franco Rubra]
Formal double, medium size flower, mid to late season, medium, upright.

C. japonica 'Lady Vansittart Blush'
Semi-double, medium size flower, mid-season, medium, bushy.

C. japonica 'Lanarth'
Single, medium to large size flower, mid-season, medium, upright.
RHS Award of Merit, 1960.

C. japonica 'Lady McCulloch'
Semi-double, peony-form, medium size flower, mid-season, medium, bushy.

C. japonica 'Lady Vansittart Pink'
Semi-double, medium size flower, mid-season, medium, bushy.

C. japonica 'Latifolia Variegated'
Single to semi-double, medium size flower, mid-season, medium, bushy.

C. japonica 'Laura Walker'
Semi-double to anemone, large size flower, early to mid-season, medium, bushy and upright.

C. japonica 'Leanne's Tomorrow'
[syn. Tomorrow Leanne's]
Semi-double, large to very large size flower, early to mid-season, medium, pendulous.

C. japonica 'Leonora Novick'
Peony-form, large size flower, early to mid-season, medium, upright.

C. japonica 'Laurie Bray'
Semi-double, medium to large size flower, mid-season, medium, upright.

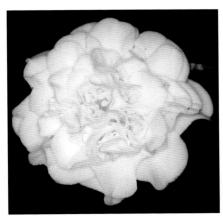

C. japonica 'Lemon Drop'
Anemone to rose-form to formal double, miniature size flower, mid-season, medium, bushy and upright.

C. japonica 'Lily Pons'
Single to semi-double, large size flower, mid-season, medium, upright.

C. japonica 'Lavinia Maggi'
[syn. Contessa Lavinia Maggi, Lavinia Maggi Imbricated]
Peony-form, very large size flower, mid-season, large, upright.
RHS FCC, 1862 as 'Contessa Lavinia Maggi'.

C. japonica 'Leonie Cowan'
Semi-double, large size flower, mid-season, medium, upright.

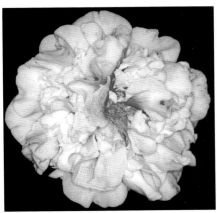

C. japonica 'Linda Brothers'
Peony-form, medium size flower, early season, medium, upright.

C. japonica 'Lipstick'
Anemone, miniature to small size flower, mid-season, medium, upright.

C. japonica 'Little Beaut'
Formal double, small size flower, mid-season, medium, upright.

C. japonica 'Little Bit Variegated'
Peony-form, small size flower, mid-season, medium, upright.

C. japonica 'Little Babe'
Rose-form, small size flower, early to late season, medium, upright.

C. japonica 'Little Bit'
Peony-form, small size flower, mid-season, medium, upright.

C. japonica 'Little Bo Peep'
Formal double, miniature to medium size flower, sometimes medium, mid-season, upright.

C. japonica 'Little Babe Variegated'
Rose-form, small size flower, early to late season, medium, upright.

C. japonica 'Little Bit Striped'
Peony-form, small size flower, mid-season, medium, upright.

C. japonica 'Little Man'
Formal double, miniature to small size flower, mid-season, medium, upright.

C. japonica 'Little Michael'
Anemone, miniature to small size flower,
mid-season, medium, bushy and upright.

C. japonica 'Liz Carter'
Semi-double, small to medium size flower,
mid to late season, medium, upright.

C. japonica 'Louise Hairston Variegated'
Semi-double, large size flower, mid-season,
medium, upright.

C. japonica 'Little Red Riding Hood'
Formal double to peony, miniature size
flower, mid to late season, medium, upright.

C. japonica 'Look-Away'
Semi-double to peony, medium size flower,
mid-season, medium, upright.

C. japonica 'Lovelight'
Semi-double, large size flower, mid-season,
medium, upright.

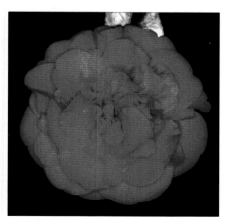

C. japonica 'Little Slam'
Peony-form, miniature size flower, early to
mid-season, medium, bushy and upright.

C. japonica 'Louise Hairston'
Semi-double, large size flower, mid-season,
medium, upright.

C. japonica 'Lucille Smith'
Anemone, large size flower, mid-season,
medium, upright.

C. japonica 'Lucy Stewart'
Peony-form, large size flower, mid to late season, medium, upright.

C. japonica 'Madame Hahn'
Semi-double, large size flower, mid-season, medium, upright.

C. japonica 'Magnolia'
[syn. Rudy's Magnoliaeflora]
Semi-double, medium size flower, mid-season, medium, bushy.

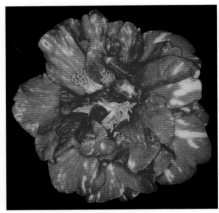

C. japonica 'Ma-Dot-Cha'
[syn. Doris Freeman]
Peony-form, large size flower, early to mid-season, medium, upright.

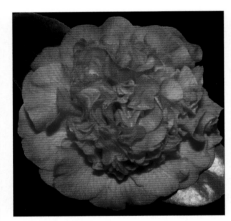

C. japonica 'Madame Picouline'[1]
[syn. Akaroa Rouge]
Peony-form, medium to large size flower, mid-season, medium, upright.

C. japonica 'Mahogany Glow'
Semi-double to formal double, small to medium size flower, late season, medium, upright.

C. japonica 'Madame Charles Blard'
Peony-form to semi-double, medium size flower, mid-season, medium, upright.

C. japonica 'Magic City'
Peony-form, medium size flower, mid-season, medium, upright.

C. japonica 'Man Size'
Anemone, miniature size flower, mid-season, medium, upright.
William E. Wylam Miniature Award, 1978; John Illges Award, 1979; John A. Taylor Miniature Award, 1979; National Camellia Hall of Fame Award, 1979.

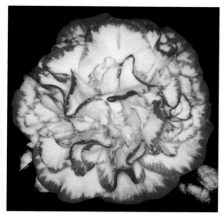

C. japonica 'Margaret Davis'
Peony-form, medium size flower, early to mid season, medium, upright.
William Hertrich Award, 1969; Sewell Mutant Award, 1976; William E. Woodroof Camellia Hall of Fame Award, 1979.

C. japonica 'Margaret Rose'
Formal double, medium to large size flower, mid-season, medium, upright.

C. japonica 'Margherita Coleoni'
[syn. General Douglas MacArthur, Campbelli, Red Queen, Tokayama (South)]
Rose-form to formal double, medium size flower, late season, medium, upright.

C. japonica 'Margaret Davis Picotee'
Peony-form, medium size flower, early to mid-season, medium, upright.

C. japonica 'Margaret Wells'
Peony-form to semi-double, large size flower, early season, medium, upright.

C. japonica 'Marguerite Gouillon'
[syn. Duc d'Orleans, General Lamorciere, Madam Gouillon, Parini Nova]
Peony-form, medium size flower, mid-season, medium, bushy.

C. japonica 'Margaret Ratcliffe'
Semi-double, medium to large size flower, mid-season, medium, upright.

C. japonica 'Margarete Hertrich'
Formal double, medium size flower, mid-season, medium, bushy and upright.

C. japonica 'Mariann'
Anemone to peony form, medium to large size flower, early to mid-season, medium, bushy, lightly scented.

C. japonica 'Marie Bracey'[5]
[syn. Spellbound, October Delight]
Semi-double to peony, large size flower, early to mid-season, medium, bushy and upright.

C. japonica 'Mark Alan'
Peony-form to semi-double, large size flower, early to mid-season, medium, bushy and upright.

C. japonica 'Mars'
Semi-double, large size flower, mid-season, medium, open.

C. japonica 'Marie Mackall Variegated'
Rose-form to semi-double, large size flower, mid-season, medium, upright.

C. japonica 'Mark Alan Variegated'
Peony-form to semi-double, large size flower, mid-season, medium, bushy. There is considerable variation in the petal shape of this flower.

C. japonica 'Martha Tuck'
Semi-double, large size flower, early season, medium, bushy and upright.

C. japonica 'Marion Hatcher'
Formal double, medium size flower, mid to late season, medium, upright.

C. japonica 'Maroon and Gold'
Peony-form, small to medium size flower, mid to late season, medium, upright.
William E. Wylam Miniature Award, 1975.

C. japonica 'Mary Charlotte'
Anemone, medium size flower, mid-season, medium, bushy and upright.

C. japonica 'Mary Paige'
Formal double, small to medium size flower, mid to late season, medium, upright.

C. japonica 'Mathotiana'
[syn. Julia Drayton, Mathotiana Rubra, Purple Dawn, Purple Prince, William S. Hastie]
Rose-form to formal double, large to very large size flower, mid to late season, large, upright.

C. japonica 'Memento'
Anemone to formal double, miniature size flower, mid-season, medium, upright.

C. japonica 'Mary Wheeler Variegated'
Peony-form, medium to large size flower, mid-season, medium, upright.

C. japonica 'Mathotiana Alba'
[syn. Blood of Christ, Inconstant Beauty]
Rose-form to formal double, large to very large size flower, mid to late season, large, upright.

C. japonica 'Mena Ladnier'
[syn. Duncan Bell, Mrs Mena Ladnier]
Anemone to peony form, large size flower, mid-season, medium, upright.

C. japonica 'Masayoshi'[6]
[syn. Donckelaeri, Tea Garden, Cantelou, English, Tallahassee, Aileen Mary Robertson, Winnie Davis]
Semi-double, large size flower, mid-season, medium, bushy and upright.

C. japonica 'May Ingram'[1]
Formal double, medium size flower, early season, medium, upright.

C. japonica 'Men's Mini'
Semi-double to anemone, miniature size flower, mid to late season, medium, upright.

C. japonica 'Mercury'
Semi-double, large size flower, mid-season, medium, bushy.

C. japonica 'Mermaid'
Semi-double, medium to large size flower, mid-season, medium, upright.

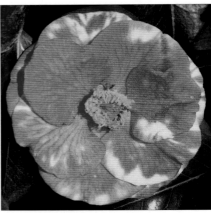

C. japonica 'Mikenjaku'
[syn. Nagasaki]
Semi-double, large size flower, mid-season to late, medium, spreading.

C. japonica 'Mercury Supreme'
Semi-double, large size flower, mid-season, medium, bushy.

C. japonica 'Midnight'
Semi-double to anemone, medium size flower, mid-season, medium, bushy.

C. japonica 'Mini Pink'
Semi-double to anemone, miniature size flower, early to mid-season, small, spreading.

C. japonica 'Meredith'
Semi-double, large size flower, late season, medium, bushy.

C. japonica 'Midnight Variegated'
Semi-double to anemone, medium size flower, mid-season, medium, bushy.

C. japonica 'Miss Biloxi'
Rose-form to peony-form, medium size flower, mid-season, medium, bushy.

C. japonica 'Miss Charleston'
Semi-double to peony to formal double, large size flower, mid to late season, medium, upright.
RHS Award of Merit, 1988.

C. japonica 'Mister Sam'
Rose-form, large size flower, early to mid-season, medium, upright.

C. japonica 'Momoiro-daikagura'
[syn. Momoiro-kagura]
Peony-form, rose-form, very large size flower, mid-season, large, upright.

C. japonica 'Miss Charleston Variegated'
Semi-double to peony to formal double, large size flower, mid to late season, medium, upright.

C. japonica 'Misuzu'
Single, small size flower, mid to late season, large, upright.

C. japonica 'Momoji-no-higurashi'
Semi-double, large size flower, mid to late season, medium, upright.

C. japonica 'Mississippi Beauty'
Semi-double to peony, large size flower, early to mid-season, medium, upright.

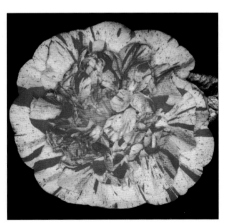

C. japonica 'Modern Art'
Anemone, large size flower, mid-season, medium, upright.

C. japonica 'Monjusu'
[syn. Numerous synonyms include California Donckelari Variegated]
Semi-double to rose-form, medium size flower, late season, medium, upright.

C. japonica 'Monjusu Red'
[syn. California Donckelari Red, Otome
Red, Shushu Monjisu Aka]
Semi-double to rose-form, medium size
flower, late season, medium, upright.

C. japonica 'Moonlight Bay'
Semi-double, very large size flower, early to
late season, medium, bushy and upright.

C. japonica 'Mrs Charles Simons'
[syn. Nannine Simmons, Nanine Simmons]
Semi-double to anemone, medium size
flower, mid to late season, medium,
spreading.

C. japonica 'Monsieur Faucillon'
Rose-form to formal double, medium to
large size flower, mid-season, large, upright.

C. japonica 'Moshio'
[syn. Flame (Australia)]
Semi-double, medium size flower, mid-
season, medium, upright.

C. japonica 'Mrs D. W. Davis'
Semi-double, very large size flower, mid-
season, medium, bushy and upright.
RHS Certificate, 1968; The Illges Medal, 1955.

C. japonica 'Monte Carlo'
Semi-double, medium size flower, early to
mid-season, medium, bushy.

C. japonica 'Mrs Charles Cobb'
Peony-form to semi-double, medium size
flower, mid-season, medium, spreading.

C. japonica 'Mrs D. W. Davis Descanso'
Peony-form, large size flower, mid-season,
medium, bushy.

C. japonica 'Mrs D. W. Davis Special'
Semi-double, large size flower, mid-season, medium, bushy. This cultivar has double the number of petals as 'Mrs D. W. Davis'.

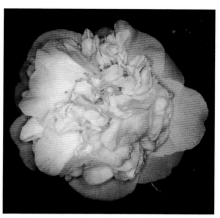

C. japonica 'Mrs Lyman Clark'
Peony-form to semi-double, medium size flower, mid to late season, medium, bushy.

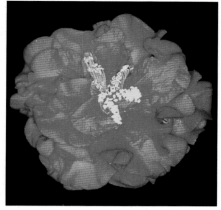

C. japonica 'Mrs Woodrow Hathorn'
Semi-double, anemone to peony form, medium size flower, mid to late season, medium, bushy and upright.

C. japonica 'Mrs H. Boyce'
Formal double, large size flower, mid to late season, medium, upright.

C. japonica 'Mrs Swan'
Semi-double, medium size flower, mid-season, medium, bushy and upright.

C. japonica 'Nancy Bird'
Peony-form to semi-double, medium size flower, mid-season, medium, bushy.

C. japonica 'Mrs Jimmy Davis'
Anemone, large size flower, early to mid-season, medium, upright, lightly perfumed.

C. japonica 'Mrs Tingley'
Formal double, medium to large size flower, early to mid-season, medium, upright.

C. japonica 'Nannie Brown'
Semi-double, medium to large size flower, early to mid-season, medium, upright.

C. japonica 'Nick Carter'
Anemone, small to medium size flower, early to late season, medium, spreading.

C. japonica 'Nuccio's Cameo'
Rose-form to formal double, medium to large size flower, early to late season, medium, bushy and upright.

C. japonica 'Nuccio's Jewel'
Peony-form, medium size flower, mid to late season, medium, bushy.

C. japonica 'Nina Avery'
Peony-form to semi-double, medium size flower, mid-season, medium, bushy and upright.

C. japonica 'Nuccio's Carousel'
Semi-double, large size flower, early to late season, medium, bushy and upright.

C. japonica 'Nuccio's Pearl'
Formal double, medium size flower, mid-season, medium, bushy and upright.

C. japonica 'Nobilissima'
[syn. Fostine, Fujiyama]
Anemone to peony, medium size flower, mid to late season, medium, upright.

C. japonica 'Nuccio's Gem'
Formal double, medium to large size flower, early to mid-season, medium, bushy and upright.
Margarete Hertrich Award, 1973; the Illges Medal, 1979; William E. Woodroof Camellia Hall of Fame Award, 1981.

C. japonica 'Nuccio's Pink Lace'
Semi-double to peony-form, anemone, medium to large size flower, early to late season, medium, bushy and upright.

C. japonica 'Oki-no-nami'
Semi-double, medium to large size flower,
mid-season, medium, upright.

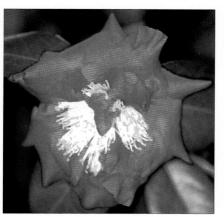

C. japonica 'Oscar B. Elmer'
Semi-double, very large size flower, mid-
season, medium, bushy and upright.

C. japonica 'Paolina Guichardini'
Formal double, medium size flower, mid to
late season, medium, upright.

C. japonica 'Omega'
Semi-double, large size flower, mid-season,
medium, upright.

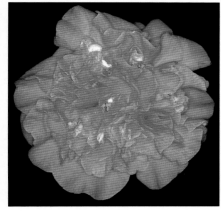

C. japonica 'Otahuhu Beauty'
[syn. Aspasia Rosea, Duke of York, Rich
Pink Paeoniaeflora, Paeoniaeflora Rosea,
Gilbeau's Pink, Stiles Perfection Pink, Pink
Aspasia, Yamaota]
Peony-form, medium size flower, mid to late
season, medium, bushy.

C. japonica 'Paolina Maggi'
[syn. Contessa Paolina Maggi]
Formal double, large size flower, late season,
medium, upright.

C. japonica 'Ô-niji'
[syn. Lady Clare Variegated, Empress
Variegated, Mrs H. L. Windbigler]
Semi-double, large size flower, early to mid-
season, medium, bushy.

C. japonica 'Owen Henry'
Anemone, large size flower, early to mid-
season, medium, upright.

C. japonica 'Paul Jones Supreme'
Semi-double, large size flower, mid-season,
medium, upright.

C. japonica 'Pearl's Pet'
Anemone, miniature size flower, early to
mid-season, medium, upright.

C. japonica 'Pink Bouquet'
Rose-form, medium size flower, mid to late
season, medium, bushy and upright.

C. japonica 'Pink Explorer'[5]
Anemone, large size flower, early to mid-
season, medium, spreading.

C. japonica 'Phillippa Ifould'
Formal double, medium to large size flower,
mid to late season, medium, upright.

C. japonica 'Pink Clouds'
[syn. Pink Clouds Pale Pink]
Semi-double to peony-form, large size
flower, mid-season, medium, bushy.
Margarete Hertrich Award, 1953.

C. japonica 'Pink Frost'
Formal double, medium to large size flower,
mid-season, medium, bushy and upright.

C. japonica 'Pilida'
Anemone, medium size flower, mid-season,
medium, upright.

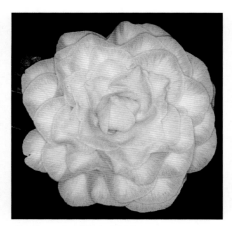

C. japonica 'Pink Diddy'
Rose-form to formal double, medium size
flower, mid-season, medium, pendulous.

C. japonica 'Pink Gold'
Semi-double, large size flower, early to late
season, medium, upright.

C. japonica 'Pink Pagoda'
Formal double to rose-form, large size flower, mid-season, medium, bushy. Occassionally becomes rose-form.

C. japonica 'Pirate's Gold Variegated'
Semi-double to peony, large size flower, mid to late season, medium, spreading.

C. japonica 'Prairie Fires Variegated'
Anemone to formal double, medium to large size flower, early to late season, medium, bushy.

C. japonica 'Pink Wings'
Semi-double, medium to large size flower, mid to late season, medium, bushy and upright.

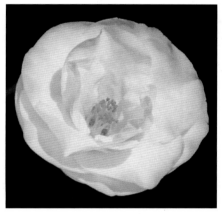

C. japonica 'Polar Bear'[6]
Semi-double, medium to large size flower, mid-season, medium, bushy and upright.

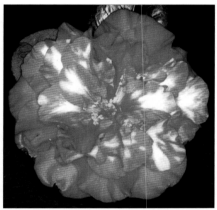

C. japonica 'Premier Variegated'
Peony-form, large size flower, mid to late season, medium, upright.

C. japonica 'Pirate's Gold'
Semi-double to peony, large size flower, mid to late season, medium, spreading.

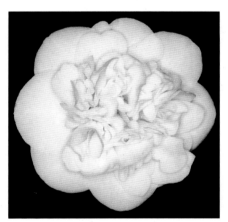

C. japonica 'Powder Puff'
Peony-form to anemone, small size flower, mid to late season, medium, upright.

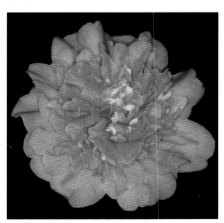

C. japonica 'Preston Rose'
Peony-form, medium to large size flower, mid-season, medium, upright.

C. japonica 'Pride of California'
Formal double, miniature size flower, mid-season, small, upright.

C. japonica 'Prince Frederick William'
Formal double, medium size flower, mid-season, large, spreading.
RHS Award of Merit 1953.

C. japonica 'Pukekura'
[syn. Pukekura White]
Semi-double to peony, large size flower, mid-season, medium, upright.

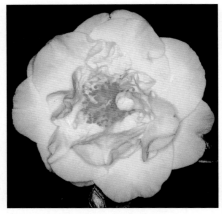

C. japonica 'Prima Ballerina'
Semi-double, medium to large size flower, late season, medium, bushy.

C. japonica 'Princess Lavender'
Semi-double, large size flower, mid-season, medium, bushy.

C. japonica 'Queen Bessie'
Semi-double, medium size flower, late season, medium, upright.

C. japonica 'Prince Eugene Napolean'
[syn. Pope Pius IX, Rosedale Beauty, Ladiner's Red, Mrs Harry Davis, Imbricata Rubra Plena, Queen of Denmark, Flore Plena Atrorubens, Conte de Name]
Formal double, medium size flower, mid-season, medium, bushy and upright.

C. japonica 'Professor Charles S. Sargent'
[syn. Professor Sargent]
Anemone to peony form, medium size flower, mid-season, medium, upright.

C. japonica 'Queen Diana'
[syn. Diana's Charm]
Formal double, medium size flower, early to late season, medium, spreading.

C. japonica 'R. L. Wheeler'
Semi-double to anemone, very large size flower, early to mid-season, medium, upright.
Garden Clubs of America 'Buckley Medal'; Margarete Hertrich Award, 1978; William E. Woodroof Camellia Hall of Fame, 1978; RHS Award of Merit, 1959.

C. japonica 'Red Button'
Anemone, miniature size flower, mid-season, medium, bushy and upright.

C. japonica 'Red Red Rose'
Formal double, medium to large size flower, mid to late season, medium, bushy and upright.

C. japonica 'R. L. Wheeler Variegated'
Semi-double to anemone, very large size flower, early to mid-season, medium, upright.

C. japonica 'Red Ensign'
Single to semi-double, large size flower, mid-season, medium, upright.

C. japonica 'Reimei'
Single, small size flower, mid to late season, medium, upright.

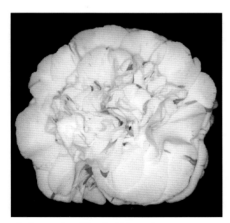

C. japonica 'Rachel Tarpy'
Anemone, medium to large size flower, early to mid-season, medium, upright.

C. japonica 'Red Hots'
Semi-double, small to medium size flower, early to mid-season, medium, upright.

C. japonica 'Rena Swick Variegated'
Semi-double, large size flower, mid-season, medium, upright.

C. japonica 'Reverend John G. Drayton'
[syn. Mary E. M.]
Semi-double to peony-form, medium size
flower, early season, medium, upright.

C. japonica 'Robin's Candy'
Formal double, medium to large size flower,
early to mid-season, medium, upright.

C. japonica 'Rose Gish'
Semi-double, medium to large size flower,
mid-season, medium, bushy.

C. japonica 'Robert E. Lee'
[syn. General Robert E. Lee]
Semi-double, medium size flower, mid-
season, medium, upright.

C. japonica 'Romany'
[syn. Belgium Red, Red Perfection]
Formal double, medium size flower, mid-
season, medium, upright.

C. japonica 'Rosea Superba'[1]
[syn. Ada Wilson, Laura Dasher]
Formal double, large to very large size
flower, early to late season, medium,
upright.

C. japonica 'Robin'
[syn. Robin (Australia)]
Single, medium size flower, early season,
small to medium, upright.

C. japonica 'Roosevelt Blues'
[syn. Frankie Bray]
Peony-form to semi-double, medium to
large size flower, mid-season, medium,
bushy.

C. japonica 'Rosemary Elsom'
Rose-form to anemone, medium size flower,
mid-season, medium, upright, spreading.

C. japonica 'Royal Velvet'
Semi-double, large size flower, mid-season, medium, bushy and upright.

C. japonica 'Runt'
Anemone, miniature size flower, mid-season, medium, bushy and upright.

C. japonica 'Saifu'
[syn. Saifu-shibori, Kyôkosode, Chûbu kyôkosode]
Rose-form to formal double, medium size flower, mid to late season, medium, upright.

C. japonica 'Ruby Mathews'
Formal double, small to medium size flower, mid-season, medium, bushy.

C. japonica 'Ruth Kemp'
Semi-double, medium size flower, mid-season, medium, spreading.

C. japonica 'Sally Fisher'
Semi-double, medium size flower, early to late season, medium, pendulous.

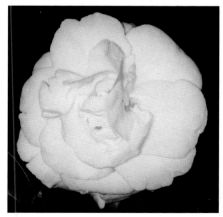

C. japonica 'Ruffian'
Semi-double to peony-form, very large size flower, mid to late season, medium, bushy and upright.

C. japonica 'Ruth McLean'
Peony-form, medium to large size flower, mid-season, medium, upright.

C. japonica 'San Dimas'
Semi-double, medium to large size flower, early to mid-season, medium, bushy and upright.

C. japonica 'Sanpei-tsubaki'
Single, medium size flower, early to late
season, medium, upright.

C. japonica 'Satanella Variegated'
Semi-double to peony, large size flower, mid
to late season, medium, spreading.

C. japonica 'Scented Treasure'
Semi-double to peony, medium size flower,
mid-season, medium, upright, perfumed.

C. japonica 'Sarah Ann Gavin'
Semi-double, large size flower, mid to late
season, medium, upright.

C. japonica 'Sawada's Dream'
Formal double, medium size flower, early to
late season, medium, upright.

C. japonica 'Scentsation'
Peony-form, medium to large size flower,
early to mid-season, medium, bushy and
upright, perfumed.

C. japonica 'Sarasa (Sawada)'
Semi-double, medium to large size flower,
mid-season, medium, upright.

C. japonica 'Scarlet Ballerina'
Semi-double to peony, small to medium size
flower, mid-season, medium, upright.

C. japonica 'Sea Foam'
Formal double, large size flower, late season,
medium, upright.

C. japonica 'Sea Witch'
Rose-form to formal double, miniature to small size flower, mid-season, medium, bushy.

C. japonica 'Shiro Chan'
[syn. Chandleri White, Chandler's White, White Elegans]
Anemone, medium to very large size flower, mid-season, medium, bushy.

C. japonica 'Shôdoshima'
Single, small size flower, mid-season, medium, upright.

C. japonica 'Shibori-Otome'
Formal double, medium size flower, mid-season, medium, upright.

C. japonica 'Shiro-hagoromo'
Semi-double, medium to large size flower, mid-season, medium, upright.

C. japonica 'Show Time'
Semi-double, very large size flower, early to mid-season, medium, upright.

C. japonica 'Shikibu'
Anemone, small to medium size flower, early to late season, medium, upright.

C. japonica 'Shiro-suminokura'
[syn. Shirasumi]
Formal double, medium size flower, mid-season, medium, upright.

C. japonica 'Silver Anniversary'
Semi-double, large size flower, early to mid-season, medium, bushy and upright.

C. japonica 'Silver Chalice'
Peony-form, medium to large size flower, mid-season, medium, bushy and upright.
Margarete Hertrich Award 1979.

C. japonica 'Silver Waves'
Semi-double, large size flower, mid-season, medium, bushy and upright.

C. japonica 'Snow Cloud'
Semi-double to peony, large size flower, mid-season, medium, bushy.

C. japonica 'Silver Tower'
Semi-double, medium size flower, mid-season, large, upright.

C. japonica 'Simmons Gypsy'
Semi-double, medium size flower, mid to late season, medium, upright.

C. japonica 'Somersby'
Peony-form to rose-form, medium size flower, mid-season, medium, upright.

C. japonica 'Silver Triumph'
Semi-double, large to very large size flower, early to mid-season, large, upright.

C. japonica 'Snow Chan'
[syn. White Elegans]
Anemone, very large size flower, mid-season, medium, bushy.
Preliminary Commendation RHS, 1964.

C. japonica 'Something Beautiful'
Formal double, miniature size flower, mid-season, medium, bushy.

C. japonica 'Spencer's Pink'
[syn. Pink Czar, Lady Spencer]
Single, medium to large size flower, early
season, large, upright.

C. japonica 'Steve Blount'
Semi-double, large size flower, early season,
medium, bushy and upright.

C. japonica 'Susan Shackelford'
Semi-double to rose-form, large size flower,
mid to late season, medium, spreading.

C. japonica 'Spring Sonnet'
[syn. Chunshi]
Semi-double, medium size flower, mid-
season, medium, upright.
William Hertrich Award, 1977; William E. Woodroof
Camellia Hall of Fame Award 1982.

C. japonica 'Stormy Weather'
Semi-double, medium to large size flower,
mid to late season, medium, upright.

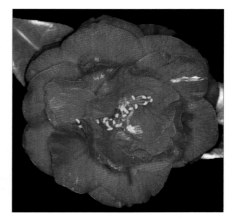

C. japonica 'Susie Fortson'
Semi-double, medium size flower, early to
mid-season, medium, upright.

C. japonica 'Star of David'[1]
Semi-double, large size flower, early to mid-
season, medium, bushy and upright.

C. japonica 'Sugar Babe'
Formal double, miniature size flower, mid-
season, medium, bushy.
John A. Taylor Jr Miniature Award, 1983.

C. japonica 'Swan Lake (Monrovia)'
Rose-form to peony to formal double, large
size flower, mid-season, medium, bushy and
upright. There is a Hybrid Camellia also
called 'Swan Lake'.
Margarete Hertrich Award, 1975.

C. japonica 'Tabbs'
Peony-form to formal double, medium to large size flower, mid-season, medium, upright.

C. japonica 'Tama Beauty'
Semi-double to peony, medium to large size flower, early to mid-season, medium, bushy.

C. japonica 'Tama Glitters'[4]
Peony-form to semi-double, medium to large size flower, early to mid-season, medium, upright.

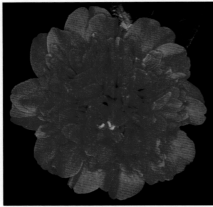

C. japonica 'Takanini'
Semi-double to anemone, small to medium size flower, early to late season, medium, upright.

C. japonica 'Tama Bell'[4]
Single, miniature to small size flower, early to mid-season, medium, upright.

C. japonica 'Tama-no-ura'
Single, medium size flower, mid-season, medium, upright.

C. japonica 'Tama Americana'[4]
Semi-double, medium size flower, early to mid-season, medium, upright.

C. japonica 'Tama Electra'[4]
Single, small to medium size flower, early to mid-season, medium, bushy and upright.

C. japonica 'Tamadare'
Semi-double, medium to large size flower, mid to late season, large, upright.

C. japonica 'Tammia'
Formal double, miniature size flower, mid to late season, medium, bushy and upright.
John A. Tyler Jr Miniature Award, 1980.

C. japonica 'The Czar'
Semi-double, large size flower, mid-season, medium, bushy and upright.

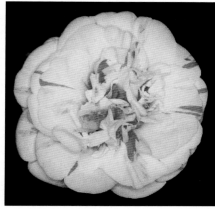

C. japonica 'Thompsonii'
Peony-form, large size flower, early to mid-season, medium, spreading.

C. japonica 'Teen Age Queen'
Semi-double, large size flower, mid-season, medium, bushy.

C. japonica 'The Czar Variegated'
Semi-double, large size flower, mid-season, medium, bushy and upright.

C. japonica 'Tiffany'
Peony to rose-form, large to very large size flower, mid-season, large, upright.
Margaret Hertrich Award, 1964; John Illges Award, 1966; William E. Woodroof Camellia Hall of Fame Award, 1978; National Camellia Hall of Fame, 1978.

C. japonica 'Tennin-matsushima'
Single, medium to large size flower, mid to late season, medium, spreading.

C. japonica 'Thomas Walter Savige'[1]
Semi-double to peony, large size flower, mid-season, medium, upright.

C. japonica 'Tinker Bell'
Anemone, small size flower, early to mid-season, medium, upright.

C. japonica 'Tom Cat Variegated'
Semi-double, large size flower, mid to late season, medium, upright.

C. japonica 'Tom Thumb'
Formal double, small to medium size flower, mid-season, medium, upright.
William E. Wylam Miniature Award, 1974.

C. japonica 'Tomorrow, Marbury's Light Pink'
Semi-double to peony, large to very large size flower, early to mid-season, medium, pendulous.

C. japonica 'Tom Eagleson'
Rose-form, medium to large size flower, mid-season, small to medium, bushy and upright.

C. japonica 'Tomorrow'
[syn. Ed Anderson]
Semi-double to peony, large to very large size flower, early to mid-season, medium, pendulous.
John Illges Award, 1956; National Camellia Hall of Fame, 1978; RHS Award of Merit, 1960.

C. japonica 'Tomorrow Park Hill'
[syn. Tomorrow Peaches, Tomorrow Sunrise]
Semi-double to peony, very large size flower, early to mid-season, medium, pendulous.
Sewell Mutant Award, 1967, The William E. Woodroof Camellia Hall of Fame Award, 1978; The National Camellia Hall of Fame Award, 1981.

C. japonica 'Tom Herrin Red'
Peony-form to semi-double, large size flower, mid-season, medium, upright.

C. japonica 'Tomorrow Crown Jewel'
Semi-double to peony, large to very large size flower, early to mid-season, medium, pendulous.

C. japonica 'Tomorrow Park Hill Blush'
Semi-double to peony, large to very large size flower, early to mid-season, medium, pendulous.

C. japonica 'Tomorrow Variegated'
[syn. Maverick, Tomorrow Supreme,
Tomorrow Tuxedo]
Semi-double to peony, large to very large
size flower, early to mid-season, medium,
pendulous.

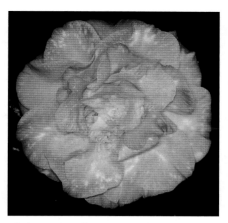

C. japonica 'Tomorrow's Sweet Image'
Semi-double to peony, large to very large
size flower, early to mid-season, medium,
pendulous.

C. japonica 'Tricolor (Siebold)'
[syn. Wakanoura Variegated]
Semi-double, medium size flower, mid-
season, medium, bushy and upright.

C. japonica 'Tomorrow's Dawn'
[syn. Tomorrow's Dream]
Semi-double to peony, large to very large
size flower, early to mid-season, medium,
pendulous.

C. japonica 'Tomorrow's Tropic Dawn'
Semi-double to peony, large to very large
size flower, early to mid-season, medium,
pendulous.

C. japonica 'Trinket'
Anemone, miniature size flower, mid-season,
medium, bushy and upright.

C. japonica 'Tomorrow's Dawn Bessie'
Semi-double to peony, large to very large
size flower, early to mid-season, medium,
pendulous.

C. japonica 'Touchdown'
Peony-form, large to very large size flower,
early to mid-season, medium, bushy.

C. japonica 'Tsubame-gaeshi'
Single, medium size flower, mid-season,
medium, upright.

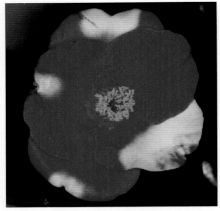

C. japonica 'Tsuki-no-wa'
Single, medium to large size flower, mid-season, erect growth.

C. japonica 'Vernon Mayo Variegated'
Anemone to peony, large size flower, mid-season, upright growth.

C. japonica 'Virginia Franco Rosea'
Formal double, medium size flower, mid-season, medium, upright.

C. japonica 'Twilight'
Formal double, medium to large size flower, mid-season, medium, bushy.

C. japonica 'Ville De Nantes'
[syn. Cody Cille, Ville (Cody's), Ville (Wike's)]
Semi-double, medium to large size flower, mid to late season, medium, upright.

C. japonica 'Virginia Robinson'
Semi-double, large size flower, mid to late season, medium, bushy and upright.

C. japonica 'Vergine di Colle Beato'
[syn. Virgine Calubini, Virgin of Blessed Hill]
Formal double, medium size flower, mid to late season, medium, upright.

C. japonica 'Violet Bouquet'
Anemone, medium to large size flower, early to mid-season, medium, spreading.

C. japonica 'Volcano'
Anemone, large size flower, mid to late season, medium, upright.

C. japonica 'Wakanoura'
Semi-double to double, medium to large size flower, mid to late season, medium, upright.

C. japonica 'White Dream'
Peony-form, large size flower, mid-season, medium, upright.

C. japonica 'White Tulip'
Single, medium size flower, mid-season, medium, spreading.

C. japonica 'Walter Hazlewood'
Peony-form to rose-form, medium size flower, early to late season, medium, bushy and upright.

C. japonica 'White Giant'
Semi-double to peony-form, very large size flower, mid-season, medium, upright.

C. japonica 'Wilamina'
Formal double, small to medium size flower, mid-season, medium, bushy.

C. japonica 'White Deb'
Peony-form, medium size flower, early to mid-season, medium, upright.

C. japonica 'White Nun'
[syn. Bainigu]
Semi-double, large size flower, mid-season, medium, upright.

C. japonica 'Wildfire'
Semi-double, medium size flower, early to mid-season, medium, upright.

C. japonica 'Wildwood'
Peony-form to semi-double, very large size flower, mid to late season, medium, bushy and upright.

C. japonica 'William Honey'
Anemone, medium size flower, early to late season, medium, slightly pendulous.

C. japonica 'Yôkô'
Single, medium size flower, mid to late season, medium.

C. japonica 'William Bartlett'
Formal double, large size flower, mid-season, medium, upright.

C. japonica 'Winifred Womack'
[syn. Bobby Guillat]
Semi-double, medium to large size flower, mid-season, medium, pendulous.

C. japonica 'Yours Truly'
[syn. Lady Vansittart Shell, Lady Vansittart Pale]
Semi-double, medium size flower, mid to late season, medium, bushy.
RHS Award of Merit, 1960.

C. japonica 'William Bull'
Formal double, medium size flower, mid-season, medium, upright.

C. japonica 'Yirgella'
Formal double, medium size flower, mid to late season, medium, spreading, yellow and green foliage.

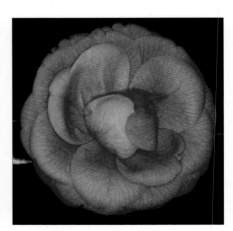

C. japonica 'Zambo'
Formal double, medium size flower, mid-season, medium, upright.

Camellia hiemalis

These camellias are mostly autumn and winter flowering, and are generally hardy, upright growers which tend to be more tolerant of poorer soils and more resistant to root diseases than many other camellias. Many camellia authorities regard this as a hybrid between *C. sasanqua* and *C. japonica*, while other scholars regard it as a separate species. It is a free-flowering type of camellia, and makes a good upright hedge which flowers well in winter.

C. hiemalis 'Goshikichiri-tsubaki'
[syn. Pink Shishigashira, Chiri-tsubaki]
Semi-double to rose-form, small to medium size flower, mid-season, medium, upright.

C. hiemalis 'Showa-no-sakae'
Semi-double to rose-form, medium to large size flower, early to mid-season, medium, spreading, perfumed.

C. hiemalis 'Bonanza'
Semi-double to rose-form to peony, medium to large size flower, early season, medium, spreading.

C. hiemalis 'Kelly McKnight'
Rose-form to formal double, small size flower, mid season, small, bushy.

C. hiemalis 'Showa Supreme'
Peony-form, large size flower, early to mid-season, medium, upright.

C. hiemalis 'Chansonette'
Formal double, medium to large size flower, early to mid-season, medium, open, spreading.
Ralph Peer Sasanqua Award, 1959.

C. hiemalis 'Shishigashira'
[syn. Beni-Kantsubaki]
Semi-double to rose-form to peony, small to medium size flower, early to mid-season, small, upright.

C. hiemalis 'Sparkling Burgundy'
Peony-form, medium size flower, early season, large, upright.

Camellia reticulata

(syn. *C. heterophylla*) and
C. reticulata hybrids

The wild form of this camellia is an open branched, small tree with large, single flowers, which may vary in colour from pale pinks to reds. They are native to the mountains of Gunnan province in China and it and its hybrids have been cultivated in China for about 1,000 years. They have great religious significance and were propagated by Buddhist monks. Over the years, many of the early cultivars have been lost. During the last 20 years in China there has been a camellia growing revival, and naming of some of the old cultivars of *C. reticulata* has occurred.

In the 1820s, the first *C. reticulata* was introduced to western horticulture, and the first one to flower was a cultivar named *C. reticulata* cv. Captain Rawes. Plants from this cultivar are still in grown today.

During the years from 1949 to 1980, many of the old Chinese *C. reticulata* cultivars were distributed in western horticulture, and these were the basis for much of the hybridisation of this species today.

They have been successfully cross-pollinated with a selection of species, with the result being that the camellia world has been given an outstanding array of many large and beautiful camellia flowers which have become very popular as exhibition specimens.

There is much work being carried out with these hybrids, and they are rapidly closing on *C. japonica* in popularity.

Although in their natural habitat they are found around the Tropic of Cancer, they are relatively cold tolerant, because of their mountainous habitat, and most appear to flower freely down to temperatures of -5°C.

They are mostly grafted, with one of the more vigorous forms of *C. sasanqua* being chosen as a rootstock. Cleft grafting is a popular form of grafting onto the understock, which is either in the ground or in deep pots. Popular rootstock are seedlings of *C. sasanqua* 'Plantation Pink', 'Setsugekka' and 'Edna Butler'.

Again, different horticulturists and keen camellia growers favour different methods and times of year for grafting, but I found the most successful time to be in the early spring, with the sap flow in the rootstock was just starting.

All of the *C. reticulata* which originated from China had Chinese names, and western synonyms. This book uses the registered names.

This section on camellias is headed as *C. reticulata*, but includes *C. reticulata* hybrids (both F1 and F2 hybrids) in this category. This is in line with *The Camellia Nomenclature Book* of the Southern Californian Camellia Society. The Camellia Register only recognizes F1 hybrids as *C. reticulata* hybrids.

Note - the flower colour of *C. reticulatas* may vary widely.

C. reticulata 'Al Gunn'
Semi-double, very large size flower, mid to late season, medium, spreading.

C. reticulata 'Alaskan Queen'
Semi-double, very large size flower, mid-season, large, upright.

C. reticulata 'Ada Emily'
Semi-double to informal double, large to very large size flower, mid to late season, medium, upright.

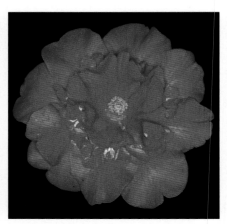

C. reticulata 'Alfons'
Peony-form to semi-double, very large size flower, early to late season, medium, upright.

C. reticulata 'Alice McCoughtry'
Semi-double to peony, very large size flower,
mid to late season, spreading and open.

C. reticulata 'Arcadia'
Semi-double to peony, very large size flower,
mid to late season, medium, upright.

C. reticulata 'Aztec'
Semi-double to peony to rose-form, very
large size flower, mid to late season,
medium, upright, open.

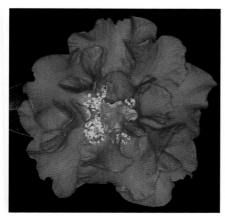

C. reticulata 'Amanda Lisa'
Peony-form, very large size flower, mid-
season, medium, bushy and upright.

C. reticulata 'Arch of Triumph'
Peony-form, very large size flower, early to
mid-season, medium, bushy and upright.

C. reticulata 'Baozhu Cha'
[syn. Noble Pearl, Paochucha]
Semi-double, very large size flower, mid to
late season, medium, bushy.
RHS Award of Merit, 1963 as 'Paochucha'.

C. reticulata 'Applause'
Peony-form to semi-double, very large size
flower, mid-season, medium, upright.

C. reticulata 'Arch of Triumph
                    Variegated'
Peony-form, very large size flower, early to
mid-season, medium, bushy and upright.

C. reticulata 'Beth Dean'
Semi-double, very large size flower, mid to
late season, medium, upright.

C. reticulata 'Bethany Fatherree'
Semi-double, very large size flower, mid to late season, medium, upright.

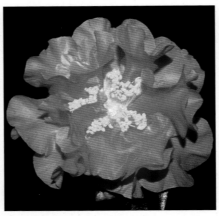

C. reticulata 'Big Dipper'[5]
Semi-double, very large size flower, early, medium, spreading.

C. reticulata 'Bill Goertz Variegated'
Semi-double, large size flower, mid to late season, medium, bushy and upright.

C. reticulata 'Betty Ridley'
Formal double, medium to large size flower, early to mid-season, medium, upright.

C. reticulata 'Big Dipper Variegated'
Semi-double, very large size flower, early, medium, spreading.

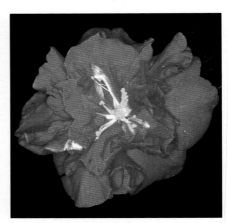

C. reticulata 'Bill La Rose'
Semi-double, large to very large size flower, mid to late season, medium, upright.

C. reticulata 'Betty's Delight'
Formal double, small size flower, mid to late season, medium, bushy.

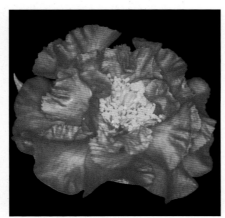

C. reticulata 'Bill Goertz'
Semi-double, large size flower, mid to late season, medium, bushy and upright, serrated petals.

C. reticulata 'Bill Woodroof'
Semi-double to peony, very large size flower, mid-season, medium, bushy and upright.

C. reticulata 'Black Lace'
Rose-form to formal double, medium to large size flower, mid to late season, medium, bushy and upright.

C. reticulata 'Bravo Variegated'
Semi-double, large to very large size flower, mid-season, medium, upright.

C. reticulata 'Bright Beauty'
Semi-double to anemone to peony, very large size flower, mid-season, medium, upright. Flower form varies considerably.

C. reticulata 'Blair Brown'
Semi-double to peony, very large size flower, mid to late season, medium, upright.

C. reticulata 'Brian'
[syn. Brian Doak]
Semi-double, medium size flower, mid to late season, medium, bushy and upright.

C. reticulata 'Brilliant Butterfly'
Semi-double, large size flower, mid to late season, medium, bushy.

C. reticulata 'Bravo'
Semi-double, large to very large size flower, early to mid-season, medium, upright.

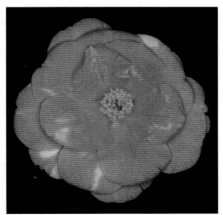

C. reticulata 'Brian Doak Variegated'
Semi-double, medium size flower, mid to late season, medium, bushy and upright.

C. reticulata 'Buddha'
Semi-double, very large size flower, mid-season, medium, upright.

C. reticulata 'Buster Bush'
Semi-double to peony, large size flower, mid-season, medium, upright.

C. reticulata 'Camelot'
Semi-double, large size flower, mid-season, medium, upright.

C. reticulata 'China Lady'
Semi-double, very large size flower, early to late season, medium, upright.

C. reticulata 'California Dawn'
Semi-double to peony, large size flower, early to mid-season, medium, upright.

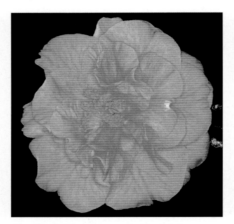

C. reticulata 'Cameron Cooper'
Peony-form to rose-form, very large size flower, early to late season, medium, bushy and upright.

C. reticulata 'Chrissie's Retic'
Peony-form, very large size flower, mid-season, medium, bushy and upright.

C. reticulata 'California Sunset'
Semi-double, large size flower, early, medium, upright.

C. reticulata 'Captain Rawes'
[syn. Chinese Peony-Flowered]
Semi-double to peony, very large size flower, late season, upright. This camellia is believed to be the first *C. reticulata* grown in Europe. RHS FCC, 1963.

C. reticulata 'Confucius'
Semi-double, very large size flower, mid-season, medium, bushy and upright.

C. reticulata 'Congratulations'
Rose-form to formal double, medium to large size flower, mid-season, medium, upright.

C. reticulata 'Curtain Call'
Semi-double, very large size flower, mid to late season, medium, open.

C. reticulata 'Dataohong'
[syn. Crimson Rose, Large Crimson, Tataohung, Great Peach Blossom]
Semi-double, very large size flower, early to mid-season, medium, bushy.
RHS Preliminary Recommendation as 'Tataohung', 1967.

C. reticulata 'Coralie Wooley'[6]
Semi-double, large size flower, mid-season, medium, upright, perfumed.

C. reticulata 'Dali Cha'
[syn. Tali Queen, Tali Camellia]
Semi-double, very large size flower, mid-season, medium, upright.

C. reticulata 'Dayinhong'
[syn. Shot Silk, Large Leaf, Spinel Pink, Large Silver Red, Large Pink]
Semi-double, large size flower, early, medium, upright.
RHC First Class Certificate, 1967 as 'Tayinhung' syn. 'Shot Silk'.

C. reticulata 'Crinoline'
Semi-double to rose-form, very large size flower, mid-season, medium, upright.

C. reticulata 'Damanao'
[syn. Cornelian]
Peony-form to semi-double, large to very large size flower, mid-season, medium, bushy.

C. reticulata 'Debut'
Peony-form, very large size flower, mid-season, medium, bushy and upright.

C. reticulata 'Descanso Mist'
Peony-form to formal double, large size
flower, mid-season, medium, upright.

C. reticulata 'Dobro'⁵
Rose-form to formal double, very large size
flower, early to late season, medium, bushy
and upright.

C. reticulata 'Dorothee Rogers'
Peony-form, very large size flower, mid to
late season, medium, bushy and upright.

C. reticulata 'Diamond Head'
Semi-double, large size flower, mid-season,
medium, upright, open.

C. reticulata 'Dolly West'
Semi-double to anemone to peony, very
large size flower, early to late season,
medium, upright.

C. reticulata 'Dr Clifford Parks'
Semi-double to anemone to peony, very
large size flower, mid-season, medium,
upright.
Frank L. Stormont Reticulata Award, 1976; National Hall
of Fame, 1979, 1981, 1982; Aubrey Harris Hybrid Award,
1977; William E. Woodroof Camellia Hall of Fame, 1983.

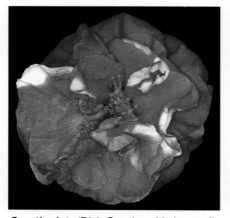

C. reticulata 'Dick Goodson Variegated'
Semi-double, large to very large size flower,
mid to late season, medium, upright.

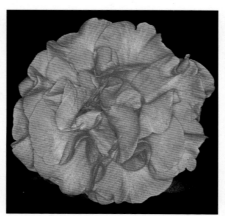

C. reticulata 'Donna Louise Timmins'
Anemone, large size flower, early to late
season, medium, upright.

C. reticulata 'Dr Dan Nathan Supreme'⁵
Semi-double, very large size flower, mid to
late season, medium, upright.

C. reticulata 'Dr Dave'[5]
Semi-double, very large size flower, mid to late season, medium, upright.

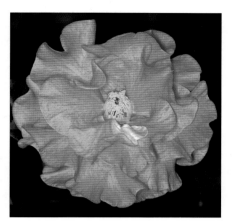

C. reticulata 'Dr Jack Davis'
Semi-double, large to very large size flower, mid-season, medium, upright.

C. reticulata 'Dream Castle'
Semi-double, very large size flower, mid-season, medium, upright.

C. reticulata 'Dr Emil Carroll'
Anemone to peony-form to semi-double, large to very large size flower, mid to late season, medium, upright.

C. reticulata 'Dr Louis Polizzi'
Peony-form to semi-double, medium to large size flower, early to late season, medium, bushy and upright.

C. reticulata 'Dream Girl'
Semi-double, large to very large size flower, early, medium, upright.

C. reticulata 'Dr Harry Moore Variegated'
Semi-double to peony, large size flower, mid to late season, medium, upright and spreading.

C. reticulata 'Dream Baby'
[syn. Little Dreamer]
Semi-double, miniature size flower, mid-season, medium, upright. Some authorities list this as a hybrid.

C. reticulata 'Ealon Magee'
Semi-double, large size flower, mid to late season, medium, upright.

C. reticulata 'Eden Queen'
Semi-double, very large size flower, mid-season, medium, upright.

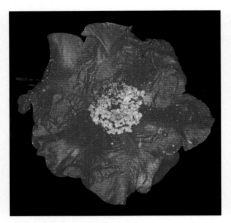

C. reticulata 'El Greco'
Semi-double, large size flower, mid-season, medium, upright.

C. reticulata 'Emma Gaeta Variegated'
Semi-double, very large size flower, early to late season, medium, upright.

C. reticulata 'Eden Roc'
Semi-double, large size flower, mid-season, medium, upright.

C. reticulata 'Elise Winter'
Rose-form double, large size flower, mid to late season, medium, upright and semi-open.

C. reticulata 'Exa Dean'
Semi-double to peony, large size flower, mid to late season, medium, upright.

C. reticulata 'Edith Mazzei'
Semi-double to rose-form, large to very large size flower, mid to late season, medium, upright.

C. reticulata 'Ellie's Girl'
Formal double to rose-form, large size flower, mid to late season, medium, bushy and upright.

C. reticulata 'Fiesta Grande'
Peony-form to semi-double, medium size flower, early to late season, medium, bushy and upright. Some authorities list this reticulata as a hybrid.

C. reticulata 'Fire Chief'
Peony-form to semi-double, large size
flower, mid to late season, medium,
spreading.

C. reticulata 'Fluted Orchid'
Semi-double, medium size flower, early to
mid-season, medium, upright.

C. reticulata 'Francie L.'
Semi-double, very large size flower, mid-
season, medium, upright.
Aubrey Harris Hybrid Award, 1969; Edward H. Metcalf
Hybrid Award, 1967; RHS Award of Merit, 1972;
National Camellia Hall of Fame Award, 1978; William
E. Woodroof Camellia Hall of Fame Award, 1980.

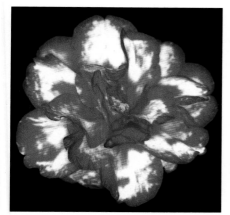

C. reticulata 'Fire Chief Variegated'
Semi-double to peony, large size flower, mid
to late season, medium, spreading.

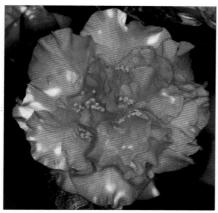

C. reticulata 'Forty Niner Variegated'
Peony-form, large size flower, early to mid-
season, medium, bushy.

C. reticulata 'Francie L. Surprise'
Peony-form, very large size flower, mid-
season, medium, upright.

C. reticulata 'Flower Girl'
Semi-double to peony, large to very large
size flower, mid-season, medium, upright.

C. reticulata 'Four Winds'
Semi-double, large to very large size flower,
mid-season, medium, upright. There
appears to be a colour variation between the
eastern and western forms of this flower.

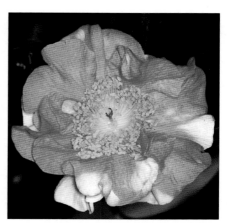

C. reticulata 'Francie L. Variegated'
Semi-double, very large size flower, mid-
season, medium, upright.

C. reticulata 'Frank Houser'
Semi-double to peony, very large size flower,
early to mid-season, medium, open.

C. reticulata 'George Firth'
Peony-form, large size flower, mid-season,
medium, upright.

C. reticulata 'Glorious Gift'
Semi-double to rose-form, very large size
flower, early to late season, medium,
upright.

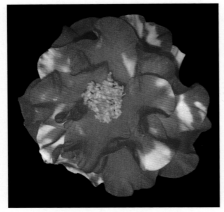

C. reticulata 'Frank Houser Variegated'
Semi-double to peony, very large size flower,
early to mid-season, medium, open.

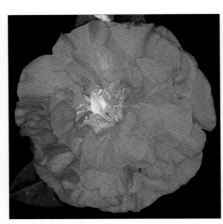

C. reticulata 'Gladys Parks'
Semi-double to rose-form, large size flower,
mid-season, medium, upright.

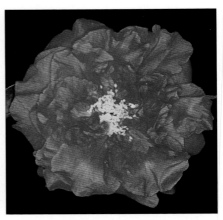

C. reticulata 'Glowing Embers'
Semi-double to peony, very large size flower,
early to mid-season, medium, upright.

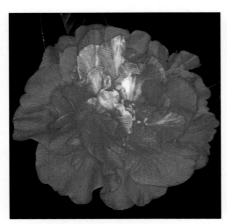

C. reticulata 'Frank Pursel'
Semi-double to peony, very large size flower,
mid to late season, medium, upright.

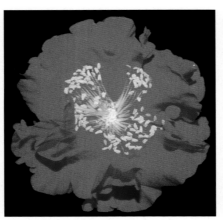

C. reticulata 'Gladys Walker'[5]
Peony-form to rose-form, very large size
flower, late season, medium, upright.

C. reticulata 'Gwen Washbourne'
Semi-double to peony, very large size flower,
mid-season, medium, upright.

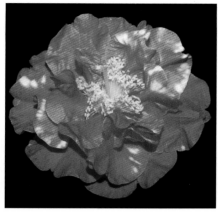

C. reticulata 'Hall's Pride Variegated'[5]
Semi-double, very large size flower, mid to late season, medium, upright, open.

C. reticulata 'Hody Wilson'
Semi-double to rose-form, very large size flower, mid to late season, medium, bushy and upright.

C. reticulata 'Howard Dumas'
Semi-double to peony, very large size flower, mid-season, medium, upright. Some authorities classify this as a japonica.

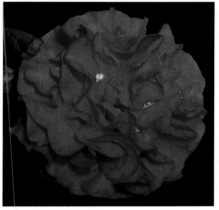

C. reticulata 'Harold L. Paige'
Peony-form to rose-form, very large size flower, late season, medium, bushy.
Frank L. Stormont Reticulata Award, 1980; Aubrey Harris Hybrid Award, 1980.

C. reticulata 'Houye Diechi'
[syn. Butterfly Wings, Thick Leaf Butterfly]
Semi-double, very large size flower, early to mid-season, medium, upright.

C. reticulata 'Hoyet'
Semi-double, large size flower, mid-season, medium, upright.

C. reticulata 'Highlight'
Semi-double, large size flower, mid-season, medium, upright.

C. reticulata 'Howard Asper'
Peony-form, very large size flower, mid to late season, medium, spreading, upright.
Harris Hybrid Award, 1963; Edward Metcalf Hybrid Award, 1964; National Camellia Hall of Fame Award, 1978.

C. reticulata 'Huia'
Semi-double, very large size flower, mid-season, medium, bushy and upright.

C. reticulata 'Hulyn Smith'
Semi-double, large size flower, mid to late season, medium, upright.

C. reticulata 'J. D. Dean'
Rose-form, very large size flower, mid-season, medium, upright.

C. reticulata 'Janet Smith'
Semi-double, large to very large size flower, mid-season, medium, upright.

C. reticulata 'Ilam Mist'
Semi-double, large size flower, early to late season, medium, bushy and upright.

C. reticulata 'Jack Mandarich'[5]
Rose-form to formal double, very large size flower, early to late season, medium, spreading.

C. reticulata 'Jean Pursel'
Peony-form, very large size flower, mid to late season, medium, upright.
Harris Hybrid Award 1985.

C. reticulata 'Inspiration'
Semi-double, medium size flower, mid-season, medium, upright.
Award of Merit, 1954.

C. reticulata 'James McCoy'
Semi-double, large to very large size flower, mid to late season, medium, upright.

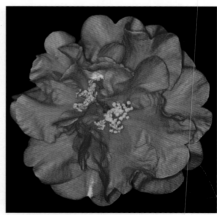

C. reticulata 'Jean Toland'
Semi-double, large to very large size flower, mid to late season, medium, upright.

C. reticulata 'Jim Rivett'
Peony-form to rose-form to formal double, large size flower, mid to late season, medium, upright and open.

C. reticulata 'John Hunt'
Semi-double to peony to rose-form, very large size flower, mid to late season, medium, upright.

C. reticulata 'Ketcam Burch'
Semi-double, very large size flower, mid-season, medium, upright.

C. reticulata 'Jingan Cha'
Peony-form, very large size flower, mid to late season, medium, upright.

C. reticulata 'Juban'
[syn. Chrysanthemum Petal, Rose Flower,] Rose-form to formal double, medium to large size flower, early, medium, upright.

C. reticulata 'Kohinor'
Semi-double, very large size flower, mid-season, medium, upright.

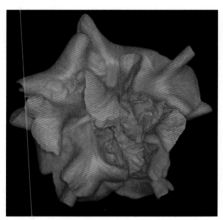

C. reticulata 'Jinxin Boazhu'
[syn. Golden Heart Pearl]
Semi-double, very large size flower, early, medium, upright.

C. reticulata 'Kathy Reid'
Peony-form, large size flower, mid-season, medium, bushy and upright.

C. reticulata 'La Petite'
Peony-form to semi-double, miniature size flower, mid-season, medium, upright, Regarded by some authorities as a hybrid.

C. reticulata 'Larry Piet'
Semi-double to peony to formal double, large to very large size flower, early to late season, medium, bushy.

C. reticulata 'Len Bray'
Formal double, large size flower, mid to late season, medium, bushy and upright.

C. reticulata 'Lila Naff'
Semi-double, large size flower, mid-season, medium, bushy and upright.

C. reticulata 'Lasca Beauty'
Semi-double, very large size flower, mid-season, medium, upright.

C. reticulata 'Leonard Messel'
Semi-double, large size flower, mid-season, medium, upright, Regarded by some authorities as a hybrid.
Award of Merit, London.

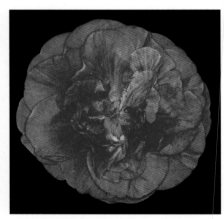

C. reticulata 'Lisa Gael'
Rose-form, large size flower, mid-season, medium, bushy and upright.

C. reticulata 'Lauretta Feathers'
Semi-double, large to very large size flower, early, medium, bushy and upright.

C. reticulata 'Leslie Rivett'
Peony-form, very large size flower, mid to late season, medium, upright.

C. reticulata 'Liuye Yinhong'
[syn. Willow Wand]
Semi-double to rose-form, large size flower, mid to late season, large, upright.
RHS Award of Merit 1967.

C. reticulata 'Lois Shinault'
Semi-double, very large size flower, early to mid-season, medium, spreading.

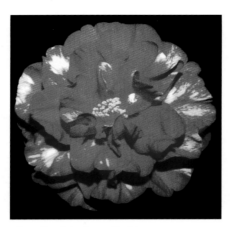

C. reticulata 'Lynette Hooper Variegated'5
Semi-double to peony, very large size flower, mid-season, medium, spreading.

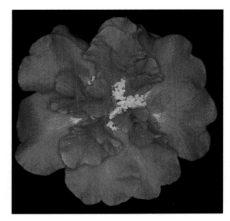

C. reticulata 'Margaret Hilford'
Semi-double, very large size flower, early to mid-season, medium, upright.

C. reticulata 'Lovely Lady'
Peony-form to formal double, large size flower, mid-season, medium, bushy and upright.

C. reticulata 'Maise Chettle'
Peony-form, large size flower, mid to late season, medium, upright.

C. reticulata 'Margaret Vickery'5
Semi-double to peony, large size flower, mid-season, medium, upright.

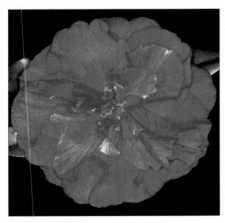

C. reticulata 'Lynette Hooper'
Semi-double to peony, very large size flower, mid-season, medium, spreading.

C. reticulata 'Malcolm Burke'
Semi-double, large size flower, mid to late season, medium, upright.

C. reticulata 'Marion Edwards'
Semi-double, very large size flower, mid to late season, medium, upright.

C. reticulata 'Mary Evans Ferguson'[5]
Semi-double to peony, large to very large
size flower, mid-season, medium, spreading.

C. reticulata 'Massee Lane Variegated'
Anemone to rose-form, large size flower,
mid-season, medium, spreading, Some
authorities classify this as a hybrid.

C. reticulata 'Miss Houston'
Semi-double, very large size flower, mid to
late season, medium, bushy and upright.

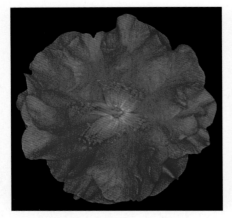

C. reticulata 'Mary Golombiewski'
Semi-double to peony-form, large size
flower, mid-season, medium, upright.

C. reticulata 'Maye Taohong'
[syn. Professor Tsai, Reticulate Leaf
Crimson]
Semi-double, medium size flower, mid to
late season, medium, upright.

C. reticulata 'Miss Rebecca'
Rose-form, very large size flower, mid to late
season, medium, upright.

C. reticulata 'Mary Stringfellow'
Semi-double, very large size flower, mid to
late season, medium, upright.

C. reticulata 'Milo Rowell'
Semi-double to peony, very large size flower,
mid-season, medium, upright.

C. reticulata 'Miss Santa Clara'
Semi-double, large to very large size flower,
mid to late season, medium, upright.

C. reticulata 'Miss Tulare'
Peony-form to rose-form, large to very large size flower, early to mid-season, medium, upright. The flowers at times may be loose petalled double.
Frank L. Stormont Reticulata Award, 1979.

C. reticulata 'Mudan Cha'
[syn. Moutancha, Peony Camellia, Peony Flower]
Peony-form to formal double, large to very large size flower, mid-season, compact.

C. reticulata 'Nuccio's White'
Semi-double, large size flower, mid-season, medium, upright.

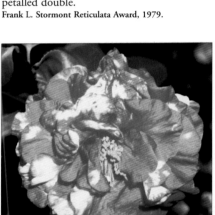

C. reticulata 'Miss Tulare Variegated'
Peony-form to rose-form, large to very large size flower, early to mid-season, medium, upright.

C. reticulata 'Nancy Reagan'
Semi-double, very large size flower, mid-season, medium, upright.

C. reticulata 'Otto Hopfer'
Semi-double, large to very large size flower, mid-season, medium, upright.

C. reticulata 'Mouchang'
Single to semi-double, very large size flower, mid-season, medium, upright
RHS First Class Certificate, 1973; Frank L. Stormont Reticulata Award, 1968; Aubrey Harris Hybrid Award, 1979.

C. reticulata 'Nuccio's Ruby'
Semi-double, large to very large size flower, mid-season, medium, upright.

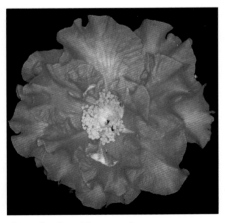

C. reticulata 'Overture'
Semi-double, very large size flower, mid-season, medium, bushy.

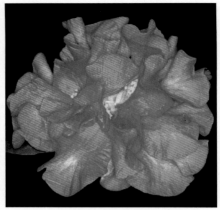

C. reticulata 'Pat Pinkerton'
Semi-double, very large size flower, mid to late season, medium, upright.

C. reticulata 'Pavlova'
Semi-double, very large size flower, mid to late season, medium, upright.

C. reticulata 'Phyl Doak'
Semi-double, rose-form, large to very large size flower, early to late season, medium, bushy and upright.
RHS Highly Commended Certificate, 1987.

C. reticulata 'Patricia Coull'
Semi-double, very large size flower, mid-season, medium, upright.

C. reticulata 'Pearl Terry'[5]
Rose-form to formal double, very large size flower, early to late season, medium, upright.

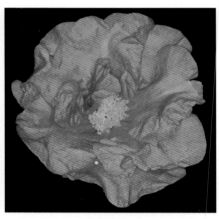

C. reticulata 'Pink Sparkle'
Semi-double, large to very large size flower, mid-season, medium, upright.

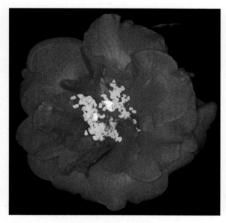

C. reticulata 'Paul Harkey'
Semi-double, large to very large size flower, mid to late season, medium, upright.

C. reticulata 'Pharaoh'
Semi-double to peony, very large size flower, mid-season, medium, upright.

C. reticulata 'Pleasant Memories'
Semi-double, very large size flower, mid to late season, medium, upright.

C. reticulata 'Pop Gee'
Semi-double, very large size flower, early to late season, medium, upright.

C. reticulata 'Raspberry Glow'
Semi-double, very large size flower, mid-season, medium, upright.

C. reticulata 'Red Emperor'
Semi-double, very large size flower, mid to late season, medium, bushy.

C. reticulata 'Pop Homeyer'
Semi-double to peony to anemone to rose-form, large to very large size flower, early to late season, medium, spreading.

C. reticulata 'Ray Watson'
Semi-double, large to very large size flower, mid to late season, medium, upright.

C. reticulata 'Renee Land'
Semi-double, very large size flower, mid to late season, medium, upright.

C. reticulata 'Queen Bee'
Semi-double, very large size flower, mid to late season, medium, upright.

C. reticulata 'Red Crystal'
Single to semi-double, very large size flower, mid-season, medium, open, upright.

C. reticulata 'Renegade'
Semi-double to anemone, large size flower, mid to late season, medium, upright.

C. reticulata 'Roberts Jewel'
Semi-double, large to very large size flower, mid-season, medium, bushy and upright.

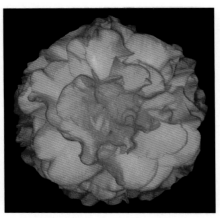

C. reticulata 'Ruta Hagmann'
Peony-form, very large size flower, mid to late season, medium, spreading.

C. reticulata 'Samantha'
Semi-double to peony, very large size flower, early to mid-season, medium, upright.

C. reticulata 'Ross Clark'
Semi-double, very large size flower, mid-season, medium, upright.

C. reticulata 'S. P. Dunn'
Semi-double, very large size flower, mid to late season, medium, upright.

C. reticulata 'San Marino'
Semi-double, large size flower, mid-season, medium, spreading.

C. reticulata 'Royalty'
Semi-double, very large size flower, early to mid-season, medium, upright.

C. reticulata 'Saimudan'
[syn. Superior Peony]
Peony-form, very large size flower, early, medium, upright.

C. reticulata 'Sandy Clark'
Semi-double, large size flower, early to mid-season, medium, upright.

C. reticulata 'Satan's Robe'
Semi-double, large size flower, mid-season, medium, upright.

C. reticulata 'Shoalhaven'
Single to semi-double, very large size flower, mid to late season, medium, upright.

C. reticulata 'Sir Eric Pearce'
Peony-form, formal double, very large size flower, mid to late season, medium, upright.

C. reticulata 'Shanghai Lady'
Semi-double, very large size flower, early to mid-season, medium, spreading.

C. reticulata 'Show Girl'
Semi-double to peony, large to very large size flower, mid-season, medium, upright.

C. reticulata 'Songzilin'
[syn. Pagoda, Robert Fortune, Pine Cone, Flora-Plena, Dobrada]
Rose-form to formal double, large size flower, mid-season, medium, bushy.

C. reticulata 'Shizitou'
[syn. Lion Head]
Peony-form, large to very large size flower, mid-season, tall, bushy.

C. reticulata 'Simpatica'
Formal double, very large size flower, mid to late season, medium, upright.

C. reticulata 'Stuart Watson'
Semi-double, large to very large size flower, mid to late season, medium, upright.

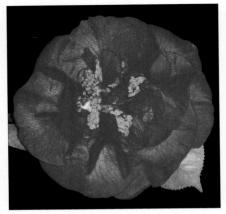

C. reticulata 'Ted Craig'
Semi-double, very large size flower, mid to late season, medium, spreading.

C. reticulata 'Three Dreams'
Semi-double, large to very large size flower, mid-season, medium, upright.

C. reticulata 'Tracey Spencer'
Semi-double, very large size flower, early, medium, upright.

C. reticulata 'Terrell Weaver'
Peony-form to semi-double, large to very large size flower, mid-season, medium, spreading.

C. reticulata 'Tom Knudsen'
Rose-form to formal double, medium to large size flower, early to mid-season, medium, bushy, Some authorities classify this as a japonica.

C. reticulata 'Tranquillity'
Semi-double to peony, large size flower, mid-season, medium, upright, open.

C. reticulata 'Terrell Weaver Variegated'
Semi-double to peony, large to very large size flower, mid-season, medium, spreading.

C. reticulata 'Tony's Joy'
Semi-double, large to very large size flower, mid-season, medium, upright.

C. reticulata 'Tui Song'
Semi-double, large size flower, mid-season, medium, upright.

C. reticulata 'Valentine Day'
Formal double, large to very large size flower, mid-season, medium, upright.
Frank L. Stormont Reticulata Award, 1981; National Camellia Hall of Fame Award, 1978; RHS Award of Merit, 1975.

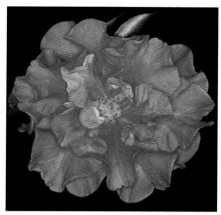

C. reticulata 'Wandin Sebire'
Semi-double, very large size flower, mid to late season, medium, bushy and upright.

C. reticulata 'Winter's Own'
Semi-double to peony, large to very large size flower, early to mid-season, medium, upright.

C. reticulata 'Valentine Day Variegated'
Formal double, large to very large size flower, mid-season, medium, upright.

C. reticulata 'Warwick Berg'
Formal double, very large size flower, mid-season, medium, upright.

C. reticulata 'Woodford Harrison'
Semi-double, very large size flower, mid to late season, medium, upright.

C. reticulata 'Valley Knudsen'
Semi-double to peony, large to very large size flower, mid to late season, medium, bushy and upright.
Aubrey Harris Hybrid Award, 1971; Frank L. Stormont Reticulata Award, 1972; William E. Woodroof Camellia Hall of Fame Award, 1981.

C. reticulata 'William Hertrich'
Semi-double, very large size flower, mid-season, medium, bushy.
Frank L. Stormont Reticulata Award 1963; RHS Award of Merit, 1981.

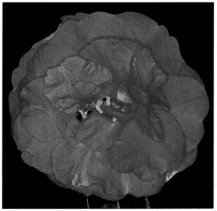

C. reticulata 'Xiaoye Mudan'
[syn. Small Leaf Peony]
Peony-form, large to very large size flower, mid to late season, medium, upright.

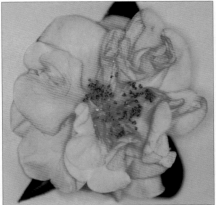

C. reticulata 'Yinfen Mudan'
[syn. Spinel Pink Peony, Pink Peony, Fenmoutan]
Peony-form, large to very large size flower, early, medium, upright.

C. reticulata 'Zhangjia Cha'
[syn. Chang's Temple]
Semi-double, large size flower, mid to late season, medium, upright.

Camellia rusticana
(The Snow Camellia)

This is not, at present, regarded as a separate species, but correctly titled, is *Camellia japonica* var. *rusticana*. The plants are usually much more compact than *C. japonica* and, because of their mountainous natural habitat in Japan, are a little more cold tolerant. They are now used in hybridization when some cold tolerance is sought. It is expected that botanists will be carrying out a review of *C. rusticana* soon, and, as a result of their findings, it could be found that this will be confirmed as a separate species.

C. reticulata 'Yinhong Diechi'
[syn. Pink Butterfly Wings, Silver Red Butterfly Wings]
Semi-double, very large size flower, mid to late season, medium, upright.

C. reticulata 'Zipao'
[syn. Purple Gown]
Peony-form, formal double, large to very large size flower, mid-season, medium, bushy.
RHS Award of Merit, 1960 as 'Tzepao'.

C. rusticana 'Beni-arajishi'
[syn. Aloha, Callie, Arajishi]
Peony form, medium size flower, mid-season, medium, upright.

C. reticulata 'Yipinhong'
[syn. First Class Red, Superior Crimson, Superior Red]
Semi-double, large to very large size flower, mid to late season, medium, upright.

C. reticulata 'Zuijiaohong'
[syn. Intoxicatingly Beautiful Red, Charming Red]
Semi-double, very large size flower, early to mid season, medium, upright.

C. rusticana 'Fukurin-Ikkyû'
Semi-double to peony, medium size flower, late season, medium, upright.

C. rusticana 'Himatsuri'
Peony-form to anemone, small size flower, mid-season, medium, bushy and upright.

C. rusticana 'Komomiji'
Semi-double, small to medium size flower, mid to late season, spreading and dense.

C. rusticana 'Mizuyoshi'
Rose-form to peony, small size flower, mid to late season, medium, upright, fragrant.

C. rusticana 'Hime-shirayuki'
Semi-double, miniature size flower, mid to late season, medium, upright.

C. rusticana 'Koshi-no-hime'
Semi-double, medium size flower, mid-season, medium, upright, slight perfume.

C. rusticana 'Nishiki-kirin'
Anemone to peony form, medium size flower, mid to late season, medium, upright.

C. rusticana 'Kasugano'
Semi-double, medium to large size flower, mid-season, medium, bushy.

C. rusticana 'Kyôkarako'
[syn. Shibori-ôkarako]
Anemone, medium to large size flower, mid-season, medium, upright.

C. rusticana 'Reigyoku'
Single, small to medium size flower, mid-season, medium, upright. This plant has attractive green and cream foliage. Pink new growth.

C. rusticana 'Sato-musume'
Semi-double, medium size flower, mid to late season, medium, upright.

C. saluenensis
Single, miniature size flower, mid-season, medium, bushy.

Camellia sasanqua

These plants are usually fast growing, very hardy and resistant to root rot. Because of this the more vigorous forms are used as rootstock for grafting *C. japonica* and *C. reticulata* in areas where these plants may be susceptible to root rot.

They are widely used as a parent for hybridizing and are usually early flowering, with flowers seen in autumn and winter.

Sasanqua camellias make excellent hedges, tolerate poorer soil, winds and sun, and are very free flowering.

C. rusticana 'Takekurabe'
Informal double, medium size flower, mid to late season, medium, upright.

C. saluenensis 'Alba Simplex'
Single, miniature size flower, mid-season, medium, bushy.

C. sasanqua 'Asagiri'
Single, medium to large size flower, early to mid-season, medium, bushy and upright.

Camellia saluenensis

These camellias are compact shrubs which are usually quite hardy. They are used as a parent for hybridizing when a compact plant, small leaves and/or white tonings are sought in the hybrid plant. They also make interesting plant as tub specimens. Many of the early, hardy and free-flowering hybrids have evolved through the use of *C. saluenensis* which has been used to a major degree as a parent plant in hybridization.

C. saluenensis 'Yume-no-sato'
Single, miniature size flower, mid-season, medium, bushy.

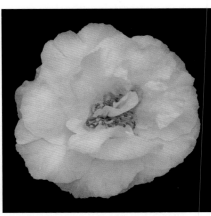

C. sasanqua 'Beatrice Emily'
Semi-double to peony to double, medium to large size flower, mid-season, medium, upright.

C. sasanqua 'Benizuru'
[syn. Pink Crane, Red Carmine]
Single, medium to large size flower, early
season, medium, upright.

C. sasanqua 'Cotton Candy'
[syn. Heyman's Pink, Hyman's Pink,
Hayman's Pink]
Semi-double, large flower, early to mid-
season, bushy and upright.

C. sasanqua 'Exquisite' (Waterhouse)
[syn. Meiya]
Single, large size flower, early to mid-season,
bushy and upright.

C. sasanqua 'Bert Jones'
Semi-double, medium to large size flower,
early to mid-season, vigorous and upright.

C. sasanqua 'Crimson King'
Single to semi-double, medium to large size
flower, early to mid-season, medium, bushy
and upright.

C. sasanqua 'Frivolity'
Single to semi-double, large size flower, early
to mid-season, medium, upright, The bud is
pink before opening.

C. sasanqua 'Betsy Baker'
Semi-double to formal double, medium size
flower, early to mid-season, medium, bushy.

C. sasanqua 'Edna Butler'
Semi-double, medium to large size flower,
early to late season, medium, bushy and
upright.

C. sasanqua 'Fukuzutsumi'
[syn. Flamingo, Chandler's Special, Zerbe]
Single to semi-double, medium to large size
flower, early to mid-season, large, upright.

C. sasanqua 'Gay'
Single, small to medium flower, early season, medium, bushy and upright.

C. sasanqua 'Hiodoshi'
Single, medium to large size flower, early to mid-season, medium, upright.

C. sasanqua 'Jennifer Susan'
Rose-form to peony, medium size flower, early season, large, bushy and upright.

C. sasanqua 'Gulf Glory'
[syn. Grandiflora Alba]
Single, large size flower, early season, medium, upright.

C. sasanqua 'Jane Morgan'
Semi-double, medium to large size flower, early to mid-season, bushy and upright.

C. sasanqua 'Julie Anne'
Semi-double to peony, medium size flower, early to mid-season, medium, upright.

C. sasanqua 'Gwen Pike'
Semi-double, small size flower, early to mid-season, medium, upright.

C. sasanqua 'Jean May'
Rose-form to peony-form, medium to large size flower, early to mid-season, medium, bushy and upright.

C. sasanqua 'Little Pearl'
Semi-double, small size flower, early to mid-season, small, bushy.

C. sasanqua 'Lucinda'
Peony-form, medium size flower, early season, large, spreading.

C. sasanqua 'Mignonne'
Formal double, miniature size flower, mid-season, small, bushy.

C. sasanqua 'Paradise Baby Jane'
Semi-double, miniature size flower, early season, small, bushy. A very compact plant, ideal for pots and Bonsai.

C. sasanqua 'Marge Miller'[2]
Peony-form to semi-double, medium size flower, mid-season, small, spreading.

C. sasanqua 'Narumigata'
[syn. Narumi Beach, Narumi Bay]
Single to semi-double, medium to large size flower, early season, large, upright, perfumed.
RHS Award of Merit, 1953.

C. sasanqua 'Paradise Barbara'
Single to semi-double, small to medium flower, early season, medium, bushy and upright.

C. sasanqua 'Marie Young'
Single, medium size flower, early to mid-season, large, upright.

C. sasanqua 'Paradise Audrey'
Informal double, miniature size flower, early to mid-season, bushy, very floriferous.

C. sasanqua 'Paradise Belinda'
Semi-double to rose-form, large size flower, early to mid-season, medium, upright.

C. sasanqua 'Paradise Blush'
Semi-double, small size flower, early to mid-season, medium, upright.

C. sasanqua 'Paradise Gillian'
Semi-double, small to medium flower, early to mid-season, medium, bushy and upright.

C. sasanqua 'Paradise Hilda'
Informal double, small to medium size flower, early to mid-season, medium, upright.

C. sasanqua 'Paradise Caroline'
Informal double, (small to medium), early to mid-season, bushy and upright, compact.

C. sasanqua 'Paradise Glow'
Semi-double, medium to large size flower, early to mid-season, medium, bushy and upright.

C. sasanqua 'Paradise Jill'
Semi-double, small to medium flower, early to mid-season, medium, bushy and upright.

C. sasanqua 'Paradise Christine'
Anemone to peony form, small to medium flower, early to mid-season, small, spreading. A very prostrate plant.

C. sasanqua 'Paradise Helen'[8]
Informal double, small size flower, early to mid-season, medium, upright.

C. sasanqua 'Paradise Joan'
Informal double, medium to large size flower, early to mid-season, medium, upright.

C. sasanqua 'Paradise Little Liane'[8]
Peony-form, miniature size flower, early season, small, bushy, Ideal for pot culture.

C. sasanqua 'Paradise Pearl'
Semi-double, medium size flower, early season, medium, bushy and upright.

C. sasanqua 'Paradise Susan'
Single, medium size flower, early to mid-season, medium, upright.

C. sasanqua 'Paradise Louise'
Informal double, small to medium flower, early to mid-season, medium, bushy and upright.

C. sasanqua 'Paradise Petite'
Peony-form, miniature size flower, early season, small, bushy.

C. sasanqua 'Paradise Venessa'
Semi-double, large size flower, early to mid-season, medium, upright.

C. sasanqua 'Paradise Odette'
Semi-double to rose-form, small to medium flower, early to mid-season, medium, upright.

C. sasanqua 'Paradise Sayaka'
Single to semi-double, small to medium flower, early to mid-season, small, bushy. Ideal for pot culture.

C. sasanqua 'Plantation Pink'
Single, medium to large size flower, early to mid-season, large, spreading.

C. sasanqua 'Pure Silk'
Semi-double, medium size flower, early to
mid-season, vigorous and upright, pink
buds.

C. sasanqua 'Russhay'
Semi-double, medium to large size flower,
early to mid-season, vigorous and upright.

C. sasanqua 'Queenslander'
Rose-form to peony, medium size flower,
mid-season, medium, upright and open.

C. sasanqua 'Setsugekka'
[syn. Fluted White, Wavy White, Elegant
Friends]
Single to semi-double, medium to large size
flower, early to mid-season, medium,
upright.

C. sasanqua 'Red Willow'
Semi-double, medium size flower, early to
mid-season, medium, pendulous.

C. sasanqua 'Yamato-nishiki'
Single, large size flower, mid-season,
medium, upright.

The origin of *C. vernalis* is
unknown, and many camellia
authorities feel that this is
not a species, but a hybrid between
C. japonica and *C. sasanqua*. Many of
the cultivars carry many characteristics
of *C. sasanqua*, such as hardiness, an
upright, bushy nature, and early
flowering. It is widely grown as a hedge,
and is, very generally, free-flowering.

C. vernalis is now widely used as a
parent for hybridisation with
C. japonica. Some growers prefer to use
the cultivar Egao as rootstock for
grafting.

C. vernalis 'Ginryû'
[syn. Dawn]
Semi-double to formal double, medium to
large size flower, early to mid-season,
compact and bushy.

C. vernalis 'Grady's Egao'[4]
Semi-double, medium size flower, early to
mid-season, vigorous, bushy and upright.

C. vernalis 'Shibori-egao'
Semi-double, medium to large size flower, late season, vigorous, bushy and upright.

Camellia wabisuke

This is another camellia of unknown origin, and many experts seem to be undecided as to whether it is a separate camellia species, or a sub-species of *C. japonica*. It is widely grown in Japan, and the characteristics are that the flowers are usually small, and rarely open flat. Many have pendulous flowers.

These plants are usually very bushy and free flowering and tend to be a little more cold tolerant than *C. japonica*.

C. wabisuke 'Shôwa-wabisuke'
[syn. Little Princess, Setchûka, Shôwa-no-wabiske]
Single, medium size flower, mid-season, medium, bushy and upright.

C. vernalis 'Star Above Star'
Semi-double, medium size flower, early to mid-season, medium, bushy and upright.
Ralph Peer Sasanqua Seedling Award, 1969.

C. wabisuke 'Beni-wabisuke'
[syn. Wabisuke Red]
Single, small size flower, early to mid-season, medium, bushy.

C. wabisuke 'Sukiya'
Single, miniature to small size flower, early to mid-season, medium, upright.

C. vernalis 'Yuletide'
Single, medium size flower, early to mid-season, small, bushy.
Ralph Peer Sasanqua Seedling Award, 1974.

C. wabisuke 'Kon-wabisuke'
[syn. Purpurea, Shikon-wabisuke, Fuyajo]
Single, small size flower, mid to late season, medium, bushy and upright, dark buds.

C. wabisuke 'Tarôkaja'
[syn. Uraku, Judith]
Single, small to medium size flower, early to mid-season, medium, upright.

Camellia hybrids

amellia hybrids are evolved by cross polination of two different species of camellias. The range of hybridization is limitless as the range of species and cultivars which can be used as parents is large.

Many hybrid camellias are produced by design with parents being preselected to produce certain features such as colour, form, hardiness, or growth, while other hybrids occur by natural means.

Many hybrids are very hardy and free flowering and may be of any camellia form, and will grow over a wide range of climatic conditions.

_C._ hybrid 'Adorable'
Formal double, medium size flower, mid to late season, medium, bushy and upright.

_C._ hybrid 'Annette Carol'
Peony-form, small to medium size flower, mid to late season, medium, spreading.

_C._ hybrid 'Alpen Glo'
Single to semi-double, miniature size flower, mid-season, medium, upright and open.

_C._ hybrid 'Anticipation'
Peony-form, large size flower, early to late season, medium, upright.
RHS Award of Merit, 1974.

_C._ hybrid 'Ack-Scent'[7]
Peony-form, medium to large size flower, mid to late season, medium, upright, perfumed and cold tolerant.

_C._ hybrid 'Anne's Memorial'
Semi-double to rose-form, large size flower, early to mid-season, medium, upright.

_C._ hybrid 'Anticipation Variegated'
Peony-form, large size flower, early to late season, medium, upright.

_C._ hybrid 'Baby Bear'
Single, miniature size flower, mid-season, small, bushy.

_C._ hybrid 'Barbara Anne'
Semi-double, large size flower, early to late season, medium, bushy and upright.

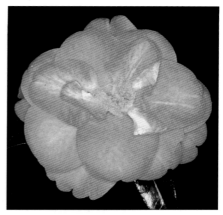

_C._ hybrid 'Bluebird'
Semi-double, medium to large size flower, early to mid-season, medium, upright and open.

_C._ hybrid 'Ballet Queen'
Peony-form, large size flower, mid to late season, medium, bushy.

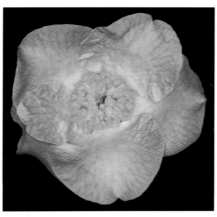

_C._ hybrid 'Bellbird'
Single, small size flower, mid-season, medium, spreading.

_C._ hybrid 'Bogong Snow'
Anemone, miniature size flower, early to mid-season, small, spreading and pendulous.

_C._ hybrid 'Ballet Queen Variegated'
Peony-form, large size flower, mid to late season, medium, upright.

_C._ hybrid 'Black Opal'
Semi-double, miniature to medium size flower, late season, small, bushy.
Champion Seedling N.Z. National Camellia Show, 1984.

_C._ hybrid 'Bonnie Marie'
Semi-double to anemone, large size flower, early to late season, medium, bushy and upright.

C. hybrid 'Bowen Bryant'
Semi-double, medium to large size flower,
mid-season, medium to large, upright.
RHS Award of Merit, 1981.

C. hybrid 'Caerhays'
Semi-double, medium size flower, mid-
season, medium, spreading.
RHS Award of Merit, 1969.

C. hybrid 'Charles Colbert'
Semi-double, medium size flower, mid-
season, medium, upright.

C. hybrid 'Brigadoon'
Semi-double, medium to large size flower,
mid-season, medium, compact.

C. hybrid 'California Snow'
Single, small size flower, mid-season, bushy
and spreading.

C. hybrid 'Cherub'
Semi-double, small size flower, mid-season,
medium, spreading.
RHS Award of Merit, 1987.

C. hybrid 'Buttons 'n Bows'
Formal double, small to medium size flower,
early to late season, medium, bushy and
upright.

C. hybrid 'Cameo Rose'
Rose-form, medium size flower, mid-season,
small, bushy.

C. hybrid 'Cinnamon Cindy'
Peony-form, miniature size flower, early to
mid-season, medium, upright, Fragrant and
cold tolerant.

C. hybrid 'Cinnamon Scentsation'[7]
Single, small size flower, early to late season, medium, open, fragrant and cold tolerant.

C. hybrid 'Daintiness'
Semi-double, large size flower, mid-season, medium, upright.
RHS Award of Merit 1986.

C. hybrid 'Donation'
Semi-double, large size flower, mid-season, medium, bushy and upright.
RHS First Class Certificate, 1974; National Hall of Fame Award, 1978.

C. hybrid 'Clarrie Fawcett'
Semi-double, large size flower, mid-season, medium, upright.

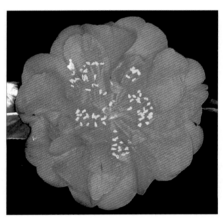

C. hybrid 'Dark Nite'
Peony-form, medium size flower, mid to late season, medium, upright.

C. hybrid 'Dream Boat'
Incurved petals, formal double, large size flower, mid-season, medium, upright.

C. hybrid 'Coral Delight'
Semi-double, small to medium size flower, mid-season, small, bushy.

C. hybrid 'Debbie'
[syn. New Zealand Champ]
Semi-double to peony, medium to large size flower, mid-season, medium, upright.
RHS Award of Merit, 1971.

C. hybrid 'E.T.R. Carlyon'
Semi-double to rose-form, medium size flower, late season, medium, upright.

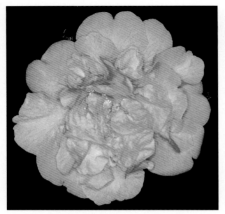

C. hybrid 'El Dorado'
Peony-form, large size flower, mid-season, medium, spreading.

C. hybrid 'Empire Rose'
Peony-form to rose-form, small to medium size flower, mid-season, medium, upright.

C. hybrid 'Fairy Bouquet'
Peony-form, medium size flower, mid to late season, medium, bushy and upright.

C. hybrid 'Elegant Beauty'
Anemone, medium to large size flower, mid-season, medium, upright, open.

C. hybrid 'Eryldene Excelsis'
Semi-double, large size flower, mid-season, medium, spreading, sun hardy.

C. hybrid 'Farfalla'
Single, medium size flower, mid-season, medium, upright.

C. hybrid 'Elsie Jury'
Peony-form, large size flower, mid to late season, medium, spreading.
Edward H. Metcalf Hybrid Award, 1968; National Hall of Fame Award, 1978; Aubrey Harris Hybrid Award, 1967.

C. hybrid 'Eximea'
Rose-form, medium size flower, mid-season, medium, upright.

C. hybrid 'Fire 'n Ice'[7]
Rose-form to semi-double, medium to large size flower, late season, medium, bushy and upright, Cold hardy to -10°F.

C. hybrid 'Fragrant Joy'
Rose-form, miniature size flower, early to mid-season, medium, upright, perfumed, cold tolerant.

C. hybrid 'Freedom Bell'
Semi-double, small size flower, early to mid-season, medium, upright. Bell shape and flowers.

C. hybrid 'Gay Pixie'
Peony-form, large size flower, mid to late season, medium, upright.

C. hybrid 'Fragrant Pink'
Peony-form, miniature size flower, early to late season, medium, upright, perfumed, cold tolerant.
RHS Award of Merit, 1982.

C. hybrid 'Galaxie'
Semi-double to rose-form, medium size flower, mid to late season, medium, upright.

C. hybrid 'Gay Time'
Semi-double to formal , medium to large size flower, mid-season, medium, upright.
RHS Award of Merit, 1987.

C. hybrid 'Fragrant Pink Improved'
Peony-form, small size flower, early to late season, medium, upright, perfumed, cold tolerant.

C. hybrid 'Gay Baby'
Semi-double, miniature size flower, mid-season, medium, upright.

C. hybrid 'Ice Follies'[7]
Semi-double, large size flower, late season, medium, bushy and upright, cold tolerant to -10ºF.

C. hybrid 'Jermyns'
Semi-double, medium to large size flower, mid-season, medium, upright.

C. hybrid 'Joe Nuccio'[4]
Formal double, medium size flower, early to late season, medium, bushy and upright.

C. hybrid 'Julia Hamiter'
Semi-double to rose-form to formal double to peony, medium size flower, mid-season, medium, bushy.
John Illges Award, 1972.

C. hybrid 'Jim Taylor'
Rose-form to formal double, medium size flower, mid-season, medium, bushy and upright.

C. hybrid 'Jubilation'
Rose-form, large to very large size flower, mid to late season, medium, upright.

C. hybrid 'Julie Variegated'
Semi-double to rose-form to peony, large size flower, mid-season, medium, bushy.

C. hybrid 'Joan Trehane'
Rose-form to formal double, medium size flower, late season, medium, spreading.

C. hybrid 'Julia'
Semi-double to rose-form, medium to large size flower, mid-season, medium, upright.

C. hybrid 'Jury's Yellow'
Anemone, medium size flower, early to late season, medium, bushy and upright.

C. hybrid 'Kramer's Fluted Coral'
Semi-double, miniature to small size flower, mid to late season, medium, upright.

C. hybrid 'Les Jury'
Peony-form to formal double, medium to large size flower, mid-season, medium, upright.

C. hybrid 'Mary Phoebe Taylor'
Peony-form, very large size flower, early to mid-season, medium, spreading.

C. hybrid 'Lady Gowrie'
Semi-double, large size flower, mid-season, medium, bushy.
RHS PC, 1963.

C. hybrid 'Little Lavender'
Anemone, miniature size flower, mid-season, medium, upright.

C. hybrid 'Maud Messel'
Rose-form, medium size flower, mid-season, medium, bushy.
Award of Merit, 1969.

C. hybrid 'Lammertsii'
Single, small size flower, mid-season, medium, bushy and upright.

C. hybrid 'Mary Larcom'
Single, large size flower, mid-season, medium, spreading.
RHS Award of Merit, 1974.

C. hybrid 'Mimosa Jury'
Formal double, medium size flower, early to late season, medium, upright.

***C*. hybrid** 'Mini Mint'
Formal double, small size flower, mid-season, small, bushy.

***C*. hybrid** 'My Diane'
Peony-form, large size flower, mid to late season, large, spreading.

***C*. hybrid** 'Olé'
Rose-form, small to medium size flower, late season, small, bushy.

***C*. hybrid** 'Mona Jury'
Peony-form, large size flower, early to late season, medium, open.

***C*. hybrid** 'Nicky Crisp'
Semi-double, medium to large size flower, early to late season, small, bushy.

***C*. hybrid** 'Orchid Princess'
Semi-double, large size flower, mid to late season, medium, bushy and upright.

***C*. hybrid** 'Monica Dance'
Semi-double, medium size flower, mid-season, medium, upright.

***C*. hybrid** 'Night Rider'
Semi-double, small size flower, mid to late season, medium, upright.

***C*. hybrid** 'Our Betty'
Semi-double, medium to large size flower, mid-season, medium, upright.

C. hybrid 'Our Melissa'
Anemone, miniature to small size flower, early to late season, medium, weeping.

C. hybrid 'Polar Ice'[7]
Anemone, medium size flower, early, medium, spreading, cold hardy to -12°F.

C. hybrid 'Rendezvous'
Semi-double, medium size flower, mid-season, medium, upright.

C. hybrid 'Pink Cameo'
Peony-form, medium size flower, mid to late season, medium, bushy and upright.

C. hybrid 'Punkin'
Formal double, small size flower, mid-season, medium, upright.

C. hybrid 'Robin Rise'
Semi-double, medium to large size flower, early to mid-season, medium, upright.

C. hybrid 'Pink Dahlia'
Semi-double to peony, small to medium size flower, mid to late season, medium, upright.

C. hybrid 'Quintessence'
Single, miniature size flower, early to mid-season, small, spreading, fragrant.

C. hybrid 'Rose Bouquet'
Rose-form to formal double, large size flower, mid-season, medium, spreading.

C. hybrid 'Ruby Wedding'
Peony-form to anemone, medium size
flower, mid-season, medium, upright.

C. hybrid 'Shocking Pink'[1]
Rose-form to formal double, medium size
flower, mid to late season, medium, bushy.

C. hybrid 'Softly'
Formal double, medium to large size flower,
mid to late season, medium, upright.

C. hybrid 'Scentuous'
Peony-form to semi-double, small size
flower, mid to late season, medium, upright,
perfumed.

C. hybrid 'Snow Drop'
Single, miniature size flower, early to late
season, medium, upright.

C. hybrid 'South Seas'
Peony-form to semi-double, medium to
large size flower, mid-season, medium, open
and upright.

C. hybrid 'Senorita'
Anemone, medium size flower, mid to late
season, medium, spreading.

C. hybrid 'Snow Flurry'[7]
Anemone, small size flower, early, small,
spreading, very cold tolerant to -12°F.

C. hybrid 'Souza's Pavlova'
Peony-form, medium size flower, mid to late
season, medium, upright, perfumed.

C. hybrid 'Spring Festival'
Rose-form, miniature size flower, mid to late season, medium, upright.

C. hybrid 'St Ewe'
Single, medium size flower, mid-season, medium, upright.

C. hybrid 'Sweet Emily Kate'
Peony-form, medium size flower, mid to late season, small, weeping, perfumed.

C. hybrid 'Spring Frill'[7]
Rose-form, large to very large size flower, late season, medium, spreading, cold hardy to -10°F.

C. hybrid 'Sun Song'
Formal double, large size flower, early to late season, medium, upright.

C. hybrid 'Tamzin Coull'
Rose-form, large size flower, mid-season, medium, upright.

C. hybrid 'Spring Mist'
Semi-double, miniature size flower, early to mid-season, medium, spreading, fragrant.

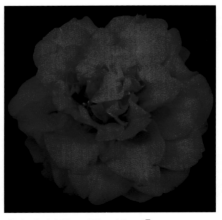

C. hybrid 'Sun Worshiper'[7]
Rose-form to formal double, medium to large size flower, mid-season, medium, upright.

C. hybrid 'Tiny Princess'
Single to semi-double to peony, miniature size flower, early to mid-season, small, bushy.

C. hybrid 'Tiptoe'
Semi-double, medium size flower, mid-season, medium, bushy and upright.

C. hybrid 'Waltz Time Variegated'
Semi-double, medium to large size flower, mid-season, medium, bushy and upright.

C. hybrid 'Winter's Beauty'[7]
Peony-form, small size flower, early to mid-season, medium, bushy and upright, fragrant, cold hardy to -15°F.

C. hybrid 'Trans Tasman'
Single, small size flower, mid-season, medium, upright.

C. hybrid 'Water Lily'
Formal double, medium to large size flower, early to mid-season, medium, bushy.

C. hybrid 'Winter's Charm'[7]
Peony-form, medium size flower, early, medium, upright, cold hardy to -12°F.

C. hybrid 'Waltz Time'
Semi-double, medium to large size flower, mid-season, medium, bushy and upright.

C. hybrid 'Wilber Foss'
Peony-form, large size flower, early to late season, upright and compact.

C. hybrid 'Winter's Interlude'[7]
Anemone, miniature to small size flower, early, medium, bushy and upright, cold hardy.

Camellias—A Photo Dictionary

C. hybrid 'Winter's Peony'[7]
Peony-form, medium size flower, mid-season, medium, upright, cold hardy.

C. hybrid 'Wirlinga Gem'
Single, miniature size flower, early, medium, spreading and weeping.

Camellia higo

Although *C. higo* is accepted to be a form of *C. japonica*, many camellia specialists feel that it may be a hybrid between *C. japonica* and *C. japonica* var. *rusticana*.

The flower forms are single, with large quantities of stamens and, occasionally, petaloids. The petals are often of uneven length and flowers are usually seen in large quantities and are very popular in Japan.

C. hybrid 'Winter's Star'[7]
Single, medium size flower, early, medium, bushy and upright, cold hardy to -12°F.

C. hybrid 'Wirlinga Princess'
Single to semi-double, miniature size flower, mid-season, spreading and open.

C. higo 'Asahi-no-minato'
Single, medium size flower, mid-season, medium, upright.

C. hybrid 'Wirlinga Cascade'
Single, miniature size flower, mid-season, medium, open and upright.

C. hybrid 'Wynne Rayner'
Semi-double to anemone, medium to large size flower, mid-season, medium, upright.
RHS Award of Merit, 1986.

C. higo 'Dewatairin'
[syn. Daitairin, Pink Fimbriata, Golden Temple, Bar None]
Single, large size flower, early to mid-season, medium, upright.
RHS Award of Merit, 1953.

C. higo 'Goshozakura'
Single, medium size flower, early to mid-season, medium, upright.

C. higo 'Higo-ôzeki'
Single, very large size flower, mid-season, medium, upright.

C. higo 'Jitsugetsusei'
Single, small to medium size flower, mid-season, medium, upright.

C. higo 'Happy Higo'
Single to semi-double, large size flower, mid-season, medium, upright.

C. higo 'Hi-no-hakama'
Single, medium to large size flower, mid-season, medium, bushy, upright.

C. higo 'Kumagai'
[syn. Higo-kumagai]
Single, large to very large size flower, mid-season, medium, upright.

C. higo 'Higo-hagoromo'
Single, large size flower, early to mid-season, medium, upright.

C. higo 'Hinomaru'
Single, medium size flower, late season, medium, upright.

C. higo 'Ôkan'
Single, large size flower, mid-season, medium, upright.

C. higo 'Shintsukasa-Sanishiki'
Single, medium to large size flower, mid-season, medium, upright.

Camellia species

The following pictures illustrate only a few of the numerous camellia species now in cultivation in the Western world. The popularity of many species has increased in the last 20 years and they are being found to be especially useful in hybridization. Others have been used commercially for hundreds of years to produce tea and oils. Many are free flowering and perfumed and may make good pot specimens.

C. chekiangoleosa[3]
Single, large size flower, upright.

C. higo 'Shiranui'
[syn. Crimson Cup]
Single, medium to large size flower, mid-season, medium, upright.

C. assimilis[3]
Single, miniature size flower, mid to late season, medium, bushy.

C. confusa
Single, miniature size flower, large, upright.

C. higo 'Shirayuki'
Single, medium size flower, early to mid-season, medium, upright.

C. caudata[1]
Single, small size flower, large, upright.

C. cordifolia
Single, nodding, miniature size flower, mid to late season, medium, upright.

***C. crapnelliana*[3]**
[syn. *C. gigantocarpa*]
Single, medium size flower, medium, upright.

C. euryoides
Single, miniature size flower, mid to late season, medium, upright.

***C. fraterna*[1]**
[syn. *Thea rosaeflora* var. *pilosa*, *Theopsis fraterna*]
Single, miniature size flower, mid-season, perfumed.

***C. crassissima*[1]**
Single, small to medium size flower, large, upright.

***C. fluviatilis*[3]**
Single, small size flower, early to mid-season, small, upright.

***C. gauchowensis*[1]**
Single, small size flower, mid-season, medium, pendulous.

C. cuspidata* var. *cuspidata
Single, miniature size flower, mid to late season, medium, upright.

C. forrestii* var. *forrestii
[syn. *Thea polygama*, *Camellia liuii*]
Single, miniature size flower, mid to late season, small, perfumed.

C. glabriperulata
Single, miniature size flower, large, bushy.

C. glabsipetala
Single, small size flower, early to mid-season, medium, upright.

C. grijsii
Single, small size flower, mid-season, medium, upright, sometimes fragrant.

C. hongkongensis[3]
Single, miniature to small size flower, large, upright.

C. granthamiana
Single, large size flower, early to mid-season, medium, upright.

C. gymnogyna[1]
Single, miniature size flower, medium, upright.

C. japonica ssp. **japonica**
var. **japonica red form**
Single, small to medium size flower, large, upright.

C. granthamiana pink form
Single, large size flower, early to mid-season, medium, upright.

C. handelii
Single, miniature size flower, medium, bushy and upright. Very dense and much branched.

C. japonica ssp. **japonica**
var. **japonica white form**
Single, small to medium size flower, large, upright.

C. japonica ssp. **japonica**
var. **macrocarpa**[3]
[syn. *C. hayaoi, C. japonica* var. *spontainea*]
Single, small to medium size flower,
medium, bushy and upright.

C. lucabensis
Single, miniature size flower, early season,
large, bushy and upright.

C. maliflora
Semi-double, small size flower, mid to late
season, medium, bushy, perfumed.

C. longicarpa
Single, miniature size flower, mid-season,
medium, bushy.

C. lutchuensis
[syn. *Theopsis lutchensis, Thea lutchuensis*]
Single, miniature size flower, medium,
bushy, perfumed.

C. miyagii
Single, miniature to small size flower,
medium, upright, perfumed.

C. longicaudata[1]
Single, small size flower, large.

C. lutchuensis 'Fairy Blush'
Single, miniature size flower, medium,
bushy.

C. nitidissima[6]
[syn. *C. chrysantha*]
Single to semi-double, miniature size flower,
mid-season, medium, upright, perfumed.
This flower varies in colour from lemon to
dark yellow.

C. nitidissima var. **microcarpa**[3]
[syn. *C. chrysantha* var. *microcarpa*,
C. microcarpa]
Single to semi-double, miniature size flower,
mid-season, medium, upright.

C. oleifera[1]
[syn. *C. drupifera, C. oleosa*]
Single, small size flower, large, bushy and
upright, perfumed. Used to produce tea-oil.

C. pitardii var. **pitardii**
Single, miniature size flower, open.

C. nokoensis
Single, miniature size flower, early season,
large, upright.

C. phellocarpa[1]
Single, miniature to small size flower,
medium.

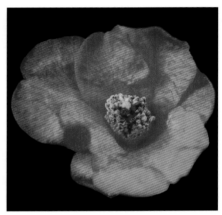

C. pitardii var. **yunnanica**[3]
Single, miniature to small size flower, upright.

C. octopetala[3]
Single, miniature size flower, large, upright,
used in oil production.

C. pingguoenenis[1]
[syn. *C. terminalis*]
Single, miniature size flower, medium,
upright, tolerant of some lime.

C. polyodonta[3]
Single, medium size flower, mid to late
season, small, upright.

C. puniceiflora
Single, miniature to small size flower, early season, medium, bushy and upright.

C. rosaeflora 'Alba'
Single, miniature size flower, mid-season, medium, upright.

C. semiserrata var. **semiserrata**[1]
Single, small size flower, small, bushy, cultivated to produce oil.

C. reticulata
[syn. *C. heterophylla*]
Single to semi-double, medium to large size flower, mid to late season, large, upright.

C. rubituberculata[1]
Single, miniature size flower, large, upright.

C. sinensis var. **sinensis**
[syn. *Thea sinensis, C. sinensis* var. *sinensis* f. *macrophylla* and f. *parvifolia*]
Single, nodding, miniature size flower, mid-season, small, bushy. Leaves are used to produce tea.

C. rosaeflora
Single, miniature size flower, mid-season, medium, upright.

C. salicifolia
[syn. *C. salicifolia* var. *longisepala, Thea salicifolia* var. *warbungii*]
Single, miniature size flower, mid-season, small, bushy, slightly perfumed.

C. tenuiflora
Single, miniature size flower, early season, large, bushy.

C. transarisanensis
Single, miniature size flower, mid-season, medium, bushy.

C. tunghinensis
[syn. *C. limonia*]
Single, miniature size flower, medium, bushy.

C. transnokoensis
Single, miniature size flower, mid-season, medium, bushy.

C. yuhsienensis
Single, miniature to small size flower, mid-season, medium, bushy, perfumed.

C. tsaii var. **tsaii**
Single, miniature size flower, bushy, perfumed.

C. yunnanensis
Single, miniature size flower, mid-season, medium, bushy.

I
N
D
I
C
E
S

INDICES NOTES

As noted earlier, the book is arranged alphabetically within each species and cultivar, but the predominant species, *C.japonica* is depicted first. The indices are arranged to allow ready navigation to each photograph.

Three indices are provided. The first lists species and cultivar, but with *C. japonica* placed in its alphabetic sequence.

The second lists the most commonly used synonyms. The genetic '*C.*' has been disregarded in terms of the alphabetical ordering of this list.

The third, the comprehensive index, is a list of all names and synonyms, again excluding the genetic '*C.*'.

SPECIES AND CULTIVARS INDEX

C. japonica (cont.)

'Allene Gunn'	19	'Burnham Beeches'	26	'Easter Morn'	33
'Althaeiflora'	19	'C. M. Hovey'	26	'Ecclefield'	34
'Amagashita'	20	'C. M. Wilson'	27	'Ed Combatalade'	34
'Ama-obune'	20	'Cameo Gem'	27	'Edelweiss'	34
'Anemoniflora'	20	'Campari'	27	'Edith Linton'	34
'Angel's Blush'	20	'Can Can'	27	'Edna Bass Variegated'	34
'Ann Blair Brown'	20	'Candy Apple'	27	'Edna Deadwyler'	34
'Ann Blair Brown Variegated'	20	'Canterbury'	27	'Elaine Betty'	34
'Ann Clayton'	20	'Cara Mia'	27	'Eleanor Martin Supreme'	34
'Apollo Variegated'	20	'Cardinal's Cap'	27	'Eleanor Martin Variegated'	34
'Ardoch'	20	'Carolyn Tuttle'	27	'Elegans'	35
'Ariana Hall'	21	'Carter's Sunburst'	28	'Elegans Champagne'	35
'Aspasia Macarthur'	21	'Carter's Sunburst Pink'	28	'Elegans Splendor'	35
'Astronaut'	21	'Carter's Sunburst Pink Variegated'	28	'Elegans Supreme'	35
'Astronaut Variegated'	21	'Celeste G.'	28	'Elegans Supreme Variegated'	35
'Augusto Leal de Gouveia Pinto'	21	'Chandler's Victory'	28	'Elegans Variegated'	35
'Aunt Jetty'	21	'Charlie Bettes'	28	'Elizabeth Boardman'	35
'Ave Maria'	21	'Cherries Jubilee'	28	'Elizabeth Dowd'	35
'Awayuki'	21	'China Doll'	28	'Elizabeth Dowd Silver'	35
'Baby Doll'	21	'Chô-chô-san'	28	'Elizabeth Weaver'	36
'Baby Pearl'	22	'Cinderella'	29	'Elsie M. Rollinson'	36
'Baby Sis'	22	'Clara Brooks'	29	'Emmalene Variegated'	36
'Ballet Dancer'	22	'Clarise Carleton'	29	'Emmet Pfingstl'	36
'Bambino'	22	'Claudia Phelps'	29	'Emmy Roos'	36
'Barbara Morgan'	22	'Cleve James'	29	'Emperor of Russia'	36
'Barbara Woodroof'	22	'Cleve James Variegated'	29	'Emperor of Russia Variegated'	36
'Bart Colbert Variegated'	22	'Cliff Harris'	29	'Erin Farmer'	36
'Beauté de Nantes'	22	'Commander Mulroy'	29	'Esther Smith'	36
'Bella Lambertii'	22	'Confetti Blush'	29	'Ethyl Rhyne'	37
'Bella Romana Pink'	23	'Constancy'	30	'Eugene Lizé'	37
'Benibotan'	23	'Coquettii'	30	'Evangelia Kalafatas'	37
'Benikarako'	23	'Coquettii Variegated'	30	'Evelyn Poe'	37
'Benten'	23	'Coronation'	30	'Evelyn Poe Blush'	37
'Berenice Perfection'	23	'Cotton Tail'	30	'Evelyn Poe Pink'	37
'Bessie McArthur'	23	'Countess of Orkney Rosea'	30	'Extravaganza'	37
'Betty Boardman Variegated'	23	'Cover Girl'	30	'Faith'	37
'Betty Cuthbert'	23	'Dahlohnega'	30	'Fancy Free'	37
'Betty Foy Sanders'	23	'Daikagura'	30	'Fannie Loughridge Variegated'	38
'Betty Sheffield'	24	'Dainty Maiden'	31	'Fashionata Variegated'	38
'Betty Sheffield Blush Supreme'	24	'Dark of the Moon Variegated'	31	'Fashionata'	38
'Betty Sheffield Coral Variegated'	24	'Dawn's Early Light'	31	'Feathery Touch'	38
'Betty Sheffield Dream'	24	'Debutante'	31	'Ferol Zerkowsky'	38
'Betty Sheffield Pink'	24	'Dee Davis'	31	'Fimbriata'	38
'Betty Sheffield Pink Chiffon'	24	'Dee Davis Variegated'	31	'Finlandia Red'	38
'Betty Sheffield Red'	24	'Demi-Tasse'	31	'Fir Cone Variegated'	38
'Betty Sheffield Silver'	24	'Desire'	31	'Fir Cone'	38
'Betty Sheffield Supreme'	24	'Destiny'	31	'Fire Dance'	39
'Betty Sheffield Variegated'	25	'Devonia'	32	'Fire Falls'	39
'Betty Sheffield White'	25	'Diddy's Pink Organdie'	32	'Firebrand'	39
'Betty's Beauty'	25	'Dixie Knight'	32	'First Prom'	39
'Bicentenary Joy'	25	'Dixie Knight Supreme'	32	'Flamingo'	39
'Black Magic'	25	'Dixie Knight Variegated'	32	'Fleur Dipater'	39
'Black Tie'	25	'Dolly Dyer'	32	'Flowerwood'	39
'Black Velvet'	25	'Don-Mac'	32	'Fortune Teller'	39
'Blaze of Glory'	25	'Dona Herzilia De Freitas Magalhaes'	32	'Fran Homeyer'	39
'Blood of China'	25	'Donnan's Dream'	32	'Fran Mathis'	40
'Blushing Beauty'	26	'Doris Ellis'	33	'Frances Butler'	40
'Bob Hope'	26	'Doris Freeman'	33	'Frances Hill'	40
'Bob's Tinsie'	26	'Dr Burnside'	33	'Frau Geheimrat Oldevig'	40
'Bokuhan'	26	'Dr Henry B. Harvey'	33	'Frost Queen'	40
'Brushfield's Yellow'	26	'Dr King'	33	'Frosty Morn'	40
'Buddy Variegated'	26	'Dr Tinsley'	33	'Funny Face Betty'	40
'Burgundy Gem'	26	'Dr W. G. Lee'	33	'Furô-An'	40
		'Drama Girl'	33	'Gayle Walden'	40

SYNONYMS INDEX

COMPREHENSIVE INDEX

RECOMMENDED READING

Literature cited for this book and recommended for further reading is as follows:-

Camellia News, The Australian Camellia Research Society.

Camellia Nomenclature, 22nd ed., 1996, The Southern California Camellia Society.

Encyclopaedia of Camellias in Color, Volume 1, 1972 and Volume 2, 1978, Nippon Tsubaki Kyokai, Tadao Tominari.

The Camellia Journal, The American Camellia Society.

The Colour Dictionary of Camellias, 4th ed., Macoboy, Stirling, 1992, Stirling Macoboy Books.

The International Camellia Register, Vols 1 and 2, 1993, Thomas J. Savige, The International Camellia Society.

The New Royal Horticultural Society Dictionary of Gardening, 1992, The MacMillan Press Limited, London.

The New Zealand Camellia Bulletin.

The Royal Horticultural Society Gardeners' Encyclopaedia of Plants and Flowers, 1990, A Dorling Kindersley Book.

CULTIVATED PLANTS OF THE WORLD

TREES · SHRUBS · CLIMBERS

ISBN 1 876060 00X

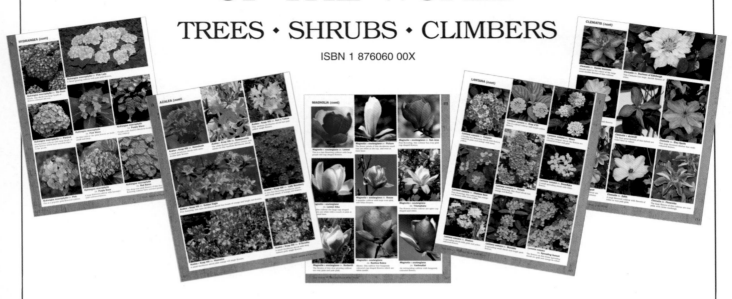

- The first and largest of the Photo Dictionary series
- 608 pages, hard bound
- A-Z format
- 4230 full colour photographs
- Pictures every plant described
- With propagation information
- With hints on cultivation

Forthcoming Publications

Don Ellison's Vines and Climbers
The Thomas Savige Camellia Collection
Cultivated Plants of the World—Trees, Shrubs and Climbers (CD Rom)
Camellias—A Photo Dictionary (CD Rom)

Flora's Image Bank

All photographs in Flora Publications are available for
use in other publications at very competitive rates.

All products available via distributors worldwide. For details of your nearest distributor, enquiries regarding distribution, or co-publication rights, please contact
Flora Publications International Pty Ltd GPO Box 2927 Brisbane Queensland Australia 4001   Phone 61 7 3229 6906   Fax 61 7 3229 8782